DARE WE OBSERVE?

For Jeannette

DARE WE OBSERVE?

The Importance of Art Works for Consciousness of Diakonia in (Post-)modern Church

ALBERT K. PLOEGER

PEETERS PRESS
LEUVEN - BELGIUM

© 2002, Uitgeverij Peeters, Bondgenotenlaan 153, 3000 Leuven

ISBN 90-429-1167-0
D. 2002/0602/88

Efforts to obtain rights from public and private collections and artists to illustrate the works in this book were sometimes unsuccesful. The author and the publisher are grateful for the use of those illustrations in this publication.

CONTENTS

PROLOGUE IX

CHAPTER 1.

DARE WE OBSERVE?

Aesthetic and Religious Experiences

1.1. Our Western Culture: The Experience Society and The Wings
of Happiness 1
1.2. Aesthetic and Religious Experiences 5
1.3. Three Phases in the Process of Aesthetic and Religious
Experiences 10
1.4. Transcendence in and Transfiguration by Art and Religion ... 21
1.5. Conclusions 26

CHAPTER 2.

LONGING

*The Spiritual Base of Certain Aesthetic
and Religious Experiences*

2.1. A Spiritual Teaching-Learning-Process 29
2.2. Performances: Koelewijn's *Cleaning the Rietveld Pavilion* 34
2.3. The Use of Rituals and Works of Art 38
2.4. The Rule of Ritual, Performance and Installation 40
2.5. Observation-Spirituality: the Role of Installation Art 46

CHAPTER 3.

DIAKONIA: CONSCIOUSNESS-RAISING

Expending Social Concern and Outreach in the Congregation

3.1. Introduction: Ways of Observing 53
3.2. Diakonia in the Bible and in Church History. Developments
in Thinking about Diaconate, 1950-2002 57

3.3. Learning to Observe Need 61
3.4. Five Steps to Consciousness with regard to Diakonia in the Congregation 64
3.5. What Follows after the Process of Awakening: Encounter and Participation 65
3.6. Towards a Congregation which Feels Involved in the Ministry of Mercy and Justice 66
3.7. Resistances and Impediments with regard to Diakonia 69
3.8. Para-Communities 73

CHAPTER 4.

PROJECTS IN DIAKONIA

4.1. *The Hidden Town*. A Sociological Citywalk as a Form of "Diaconal" Observing 79
4.2. "*I have nobody*". The Silent Help. Solitude, Handicap and the Work of Deacons 86
4.3. Open Houses for the Lonely or Homeless 89
4.4. *Presence*: A Way of Social Attentiveness 100
4.5. Exposure 103
4.6. "AZC": State Refugee Centres and the Way Deacons Observe the Human Right to Live in Freedom 104

CHAPTER 5.

AESTHETIC INSTALLATIONS

5.1. Dare to Observe! Examples in a Nutshell: Beuys, Acconci et al. 108
5.2. An Elaborate Example: Mathilde ter Heijne, *Life inside storage* 121
5.3. Experiencing Aesthetic Installations 127
5.4. Awareness of Diakonia and Aesthetic Installations 130

CHAPTER 6.

THE COURAGE TO OBSERVE

*The Importance of Performance and Installation Art for Christian
Education and its Tasks of Expanding Social Concern
and Outreach in the Congregation*

6.1. The Basis 134
6.2. Using Performances and Installations to Further Consciousness
     regarding Diakonia: Study Group 'k.o.9' Autumn 2001 138
6.3. Becoming Part of the Scene: Longing for a Safe Home for all
     Human beings... 151

NOTES 156

LIST OF ARTISTS AND THEIR WORKS 173

LIST OF ILLUSTRATIONS 175

PROLOGUE

A Dutch Christian's Reverie

Once upon a time righteous, good, wise and cheerful gods made the cosmos. Their names were, among others, Buddha, Adonai, Krishna, Jesus, Allah, Tecumseh and Humanity. The gods made the cosmos and, as part of it, they made the earth, full of life, plants, animals and people.

The gods liked to play with men and women. They taught them to play together the game of justice and wisdom, the game of love, the game of joy and happiness. But gradually human beings invented their own playmates, and in the end the gods no longer paid attention to the earth. People threw themselves away on playing with science and technology, playing with power, weapons and money. To humiliate, impoverish, starve or kill the rival once and for all was the new game.

Finally everybody on earth, clever or dull, poor or rich, knew the rules of the game of power. It became everybody's game, so everybody lost.
Now people tried to retrace their steps, back to the true gods who were so righteous, good, wise and cheerful. But they had lost their ability to see them.

One day, while making their way through the cosmos, Buddha, Adonai, Krishna, Jesus, Allah, Tecumseh, Humanity and the rest of the gods heard a weak, fading crying. They said to each other: "What on earth is going on there...."

Their voices echoed through universe and even reached the ravaged human beings on earth. Do human beings hear the gods? Do they listen to those righteous, good, wise and cheerful voices? Dare they change? Dare they observe?

About this book

We live in the information era, within the experience society. I call our time (post-)modern[1]. Most people in Western society, and especially state and technological domains such as medicine, industry and business, think in a late-modern way. But shocks about the relativity of our knowledge and the instability of our culture, questions about gender and sexual status, together with ongoing streams of information and an inexhaustible supply of entertainment, form the background of postmodern thinking in philosophy and religion. Therefore I prefer a term that reflects both the modern and postmodern features of our culture: (post-)modern.

In the information era, we have access to views on every culture by means of radio, television, cell phones and the Internet. The norms, values and insights of people who are open to the world are changing all the time owing to streams of new information. As I write this, we are being offered more, and more varied, information on Islam than ever before, and many people are changing their beliefs about Muslims, whether in a positive or a negative direction. In a more general way we are called on to react to new insights and possibilities in the domains of health care, employment and recreation, as well as to a constantly changing spectrum of religious views, philosophies and political doctrines.

Owing to technological progress most people in the West are relatively wealthy and have fulfilled their lust to maximize sheer income[2]. They have a great deal of spare time to explore fields of personal interest and to live out subjective, postmaterial values. Most are engaged in an egocentric search for happiness, but perhaps they will discover that happiness can be found in a social commitment that goes beyond ego, family and best friends[3].

This book is about Christian faith and the Christian congregation in the information era, within the experience society. It is my opinion that Christians like me who want to participate in the (post-)modern culture have to answer two questions.

- What is the core, the essence, of the Christian tradition, the reason why people in a (post-)modern culture continue to be deeply affected by it?
- How can we interpret this core of Christian tradition in our (post-)modern time, for people living in the information-loaded and experientially-focused society, so that they will long to live with this tradition?

It is characteristic of (post-)modern thinking and feeling that we cannot solve these questions to the satisfaction of everybody. In our society everyone is free to feel and think about religion and world view as he or she wishes. Similarly, the (post-)modern congregation is free and open. Therefore I can only give my personal presuppositions, as a believer and as a theologian, to both questions. And because in the present book I write about only an aspect of both questions, I will confine myself to some words about what I call my believing-theological standpoint.

To me the core of contemporary Christian theology and faith consists of elements from the story of women and men in Israel, and especially of the Jew Jesus, as worked out in Christian tradition. The elements of this tradition, as it can be understood today, have three traits in common.

First, this tradition is about experiences these women and men had in their everyday lives, either profane or religious, that went beyond their 'normal' ways of material and mental feeling and thinking in a mysterious, what we might call spiritual way, and that they named 'revelation' or 'relatedness to the God of Israel' – in Christian terms: revelation by the Holy Ghost.

Second, this tradition tells in a human, understandable way, how God acts. We especially see God's action in the life and death of Jesus, the mark of our reconciliation, and in the history of the faithful in Israel and the church. In them we see God's 'care for every subject', not least the poor and the wretched, connoted by words like trust in God and in life, love, freedom, righteousness, grace, integrity.

Third, this tradition expresses the possibilities and impossibilities of living and acting in a covenant with God today. Like Jesus and the other faithful in Israel and the church in history, we can, helped by the Holy Spirit, act as God would act if God were a human being.

Thus we foresee the Kingdom of God, partially now, but in fullness one day.

I speak of "elements of the tradition", for already in the Bible one finds irreconcilable teachings and conclusions in different situations, and the Christian tradition makes clear that the same goes for people in other ages. This is especially evident in our time. An individual, and (post-)modern people in general, cannot grasp every word and every meaning in the Bible. Each of us can only understand and 'believe' the Word of God as it fits in with our personality, our nature and our nurturing, and the contemporary context. That is why I stress the need for *reciprocal hermeneutics*.

"*Hermeneutics A*", often called biblical theology and dogmatics, implies the interpretation of Bible and tradition for (post-)modern people. "*Hermeneutics B*", as realized in practical-theological research but also in practice, implies the interpretation of contemporary faith, beliefs of all kinds (often called devotion and even superstition) and action of Christians as well as others. To me these two hermeneutics must test each other. Theology has no preference over the lived faith. I believe that God's Spirit created the world and humankind, and that it has worked in human beings to this day, as was recognized in Israel and in the Christian church. Not only does the Spirit help us to remember the care God showed for humankind in Israel and in Jesus Christ, but it awakens us to seek to live in the image of God, waiting and living for the Kingdom. In our informational and experience society this means 'taking pleasure in God and enjoying life as much as possible, and looking after every suffering creature on earth'.

These intentions I call 'leitourgia' and 'diakonia', the old Greek words for two classic functions of the church that have a normative meaning. Leitourgia means serving God through prayer, praise, and enjoyment of His presence, to which I add the enjoyment of creation, and all of the material and intellectual goods we are blessed with. Diakonia means the willingness to be a companion to, to stand with those who suffer more than a human being can bear.

Two other traditional church functions are marturia and koinonia. Marturia – or kerugma – is the proclamation of the Gospel, in church and mission. This function is 'hidden' in the reciprocal hermeneutics mentioned before. I connect the koinonia function, which is often placed first, with leitourgia and diakonia. In most congregations there is plenty of singing and praising the Lord. But, as Jesus said, "Not everyone who calls 'Lord, Lord', will enter the kingdom of Heaven, but only those who do the will of my heavenly Father" (Matthew 7,21). The intertwining of leitourgia and diakonia determines whether a congregation may call itself a koinonia of Christ[4]. The words 'community' or 'congregation' are free to be used by all; the term 'body of Christ' is given to the church by the grace of God; but koinonia, as a normative function, must be enacted.

The need for diakonia in an open and free congregation of (post)modern people, and ways in which it can be brought into being, are the subject of this study. I will suggest that Christians in the experience society can learn much about diakonia and the corresponding attitude from postmodern aesthetics and recent philosophy of art, even though most church members normally have no eye for art, let alone postmodern art[5].

The keyword is aisthesis, 'observing', versus amnesia, 'the always forgotten'[6]. Do we dare to really open our eyes – as artists do – and look around us at the world? If we do, if we have the courage to observe, we will see what 'being looked after' by God can mean for our own lives. We will have an eye for those who are suffering because of injustice and hatred in our world; we will see in a different light what is going on in our society. Dare we open our eyes and mind? Dare we observe?

Acknowledgements

This book includes, as Chapter 6, the English version of the valedictory lecture I gave as professor of Practical Theology and Religious Education at Groningen University on June 25, 2002.

I dedicate this book to my wife Jeannette, who opened my eyes for diakonia.

I thank the Reformed Theological Academic Institute (HTWI) for financial assistance, Barbara Schultz for the correction of the text and my collegue Rick Osmer in Princeton for scientific help.

Groningen/Steggerda, 3/19/2002   A.K.P.

Chapter 1

DARE WE OBSERVE?
Aesthetic and Religious Experiences

1.1. Our Western Culture: The Experience Society and The Wings of Happiness

"*The Experience Society*", "die Erlebnisgesellschaft", is the phrase coined by German sociologist Gerhard Schulze in his book of the same name[1] to characterize our western lifeworld. The key to this society, according to Schulze, is "the idea that we can shape a pleasant, interesting life that we subjectively find rewarding". The experience society is increasingly inward-oriented. Thinking is directed toward goals in people themselves, toward feelings, experiences, achieving happiness. The old social classes become "milieus", people are attracted to others because of their personal style, age or education, and for how they "manage" their own situation. In the experiential society, a person's identity is no longer a given. No longer are we defined by birth, trade, living and religion, but each one of us has to search for his or her own identity. As Schulze says, "One of the particularities of today's cultural-historic period is the unclearness of the self for one's self".

In his extensive research conducted in Germany, Schulze found that people under the age of forty (now, ten years after his book was published, we would presumably say under the age of fifty) belong to either the milieu of self-realization or to the milieu of (self-chosen) entertainment. However, freedom to choose does not make people psychologically more stable. Many experiences end in disappointment, and lead to boredom and not to happiness.

Schulze believes that we can only live between what he calls the "wings of happiness"[2]. These, he says, are of two kinds: lying wings and playful wings. The first kind are used to cover up things we would prefer to hide. An example might be a park located between a wealthy neighbourhood and poorer ones. Playful wings, on the other hand, for example theme parks, computer games or movies, he describes as "illusion-evoking constructions" in which feelings, fantasies and experiences are not, as they are in the lying wings, seen as disturbances of observing, but as a reality in its own right.

Discourse into what constitutes the beautiful life, the nature of the wings of happiness, goes on everywhere from fitness centre to the talkshow, from conversations in the supermarket to coffee breaks at the workplace and recess on the playground, not to mention in the office and classroom themselves. In considering the wings of happiness, Schulze says, we raise two kinds of questions. The first is the old Aristotelean question "How do I avoid unhappiness?" and the other, which Aristotle concluded should be dropped altogether is "How do I achieve happiness?" The first question directs us toward rather concrete problems such as illness, poverty and powerlessness. Especially in wealthy countries, we have the means to reduce the likelihood of being ill, poor or powerless. There are things we can do to avoid or alleviate unhappiness. The second question is much more difficult to answer, for it concerns primarily our inner life. Schulze calls the "wings of happiness" scenarios of a possible and elective inner life, communally created and developed planes of projection for feelings, wishes and fantasies, for human nature. As Schulze notes, "a basic theatrical concept has leaped over to the whole of everyday life; wings are now present everywhere". No longer obliged to work all the time, people are now free to stage part of their lives; they have the money and the means to devote their free time to playful wings that promise happiness. What children have always done, staging their life from game to game, adults today can also do. In fact they need to, for the wings have become part of our world. In former times people were devoured by the daily struggle for survival. Today people in the West have free time and money, as well as a vast supply of goods, services and entertainment from which they are expected to choose "events". From these freely chosen events they expect to gain feelings of happiness and the development of their own subjective identity.

Walter Benjamin, before World War II, wrote about the "aestheticization of the life-world" and Schulze, like others, has picked up this phrase. Schulze speaks of what he calls the "everyday aesthetic" ("Alltagsästhetik"), the project of the beautiful life[3].

But the beautiful life cannot be realized if people remain fixed in an inwardly oriented attitude. It is necessary also to try to acquire "the competence to engage in something other", beyond the experience of events, "and always again also beyond oneself". This means: inner life requires social interaction.

People also need an outward orientation. They need to define goals for action in outer life[4]. Thus the part of society which Schulze calls the experience society is not the whole of society. Schulze seeks a kind of equilibrium between the external world, i.e. the actions of people in the world, their discourse with one another, the know-how and know-of each of us needs in order to meet our material needs, and the inner-orientation that characterizes the experience society.

Event Culture and Diaconate

Schulze's key concept of 'events', based on one of his empirically confirmed hypotheses, merits discussion. Schulze argues that an event is not based on the old idea of three predetermined spheres – "one experiences; one experiences communally; one experiences something 'real'"[5] – in which the three spheres of the subjective, the intersubjective and the objective worked together. Today, says Schulze, this scheme is related only to the single person, and not to a group of people experiencing an event. An individual experiencing an event, even a communal one such as religious worship, through his senses, may feel good personally and even have feelings of community and of sharing a common belief with others; another person experiencing the same event may also have subjective, intersubjective and objective feelings in the same way; and yet, if the two individuals were to talk about the experience, it would turn out that their feelings about it were quite different.

My aim in the following is to try to connect the *external* world of church, faith and needs or actions with regard to diakonia, which I propose to call a kind of being-with-God, with Schulze's ideas about the individual experience of personal *inner life*, which I also call a kind of being-with-God. Therefore Schulze's empirical finding, as expressed in the preceding paragraph, is important. If Schulze is right, we celebrate together in religious worship and we act together in projects in the ministry of mercy and justice, but we do not really have the same feelings and subjective impressions of these events. Is this true? When we discuss a sermon, or the content of a project, are our feelings and responses personal and different from those of others – even when we, as Schulze advises, step outside the circularity of the event culture and acquire the competence to engage in something otherwise? According to Schulze the true art of living, which consists of a mixture of experiencing events and forgetting oneself, always remains a personal matter.

Certainly, modern and post-modern people are highly individualized and their identities fragmented. But surely two or more people can, in some of their fragments of identity, feel bound together by common responses and shared feelings. If such a sense of 'relatedness' exists, it would surely be in the fields of religion and art.

So I suggest a link between the event-world of an individual person and his social world, shared with others by intersubjective discussions. Religion and art are part of the event-world. But they can incite people to work towards a better world. The German philosopher Welsch would ascribe such links to transversal reason[6], as we will see below.

In the following chapters on religion, art and diaconate, I will take as my starting point the empirical situation of an experiential society. It is true that people today want to experience life, and religious life as well, in a subjective way. Religion is after all more than an objective belief in the Bible and in traditional dogmas. It is about seeing the Unseen who awakens love and righteousness, and demands much more than our normal mode of objective, analytical observation.

Our 'normal' mode of observation of reality is determined by our nature, our socialization, our biography and our contemporary life context.

Owing to our acquaintance with other people and what we know about their ideas, feelings and observations, we are aware that our frame of reference does not show us 'reality as it really is'. We can, to some extent, broaden our understanding and change our mind by learning and intersubjective communication, by listening, by observing others. But expanding our mode of observation is much more than changing our cognitive thinking. The kind of observation, or aisthesis, I want to promote involves becoming more conscious of personal identity (a psychological process of coping with anxieties, sublimation and so on), of cultural context (awareness of connections and differences between one's own lifeworld and that of others), and of possible coherence between one's own faith and other aspects of one's experience of reality, for example in social, political and economic domains. In this way we might see everyday events as a whole, with immanent and transcendent aspects. For instance, we could make connections between our work, or what we see on television and the Internet, and our faith commitments, specifically, for the purpose of the present discussion, diakonia and observing people who suffer more than they can bear.

Religion and theology today need aisthesis, observing in the fullest sense, and therefore a plurality of critical aesthetic approaches is called for. In this respect theologians and believers can learn much from modern as well as post-modern aesthetic theories[7].

For this reason the present chapter continues with an introduction to the common sources of religious and aesthetic experiences. In Chapter 2 I set about explaining the idea of longing as the spiritual basis of certain aesthetic and religious experiences. After that I introduce the subject diaconate, good and righteous action, which is compared and contrasted in the rest of the book with these aesthetic and religious experiences, and leads ultimately to the intended teaching/learning process about diakonia.

1.2. Aesthetic and Religious Experiences[8]

What is religion? What is art? What do they have in common?

In recent years I have come across a number of catchwords or phrases that appear to me to express a relation between religion, morality and art, be it the absorbing of religion into morality and art, or even the overtaking of religion, morality and art by enjoyment. These are phrases such as the "aestheticization of the life-world" (Benjamin; Baudrillard; Bubner), "people with a multi-medial identity" (Baudrillard, Münch), De Mul and Schulze's aforementioned "experience society" or "event culture"[9]

A very subjective, spiritual observation...

Some years ago, as I climbed the stairs of the Stedelijk Museum in Amsterdam, my attention was caught by a drawing. That I would be interested in a drawing was quite understandable, for I was a draughtsman for twelve years in my former life.

This was a very special drawing, however. It did not represent a building – a factory, house, office or even a theatre. No, this was a gate, a heavy gate with a most peculiar handle. The handle could be used to open the gate and pass through to the inside. But there is no inside. There is merely a heavy gate, and a most peculiar handle.

I read that this work was by the Austrian sculptor Walter Pichler. Touched as much by the drawing as by my own memories, I walked to the next hall, and found myself looking with astonishment at the Holy Trinity (figure 1.1).

Three staffs, cut from one solid block of hardwood; two of them, about four inches in diameter, lying side by side, and the third, about three inches in diameter, on top. All three about four feet long, atop a gigantic block of oak measuring more than three feet wide by three feet high, and ten feet long.

That huge block, I thought to myself, is the earth where people live, and where the Father and the Son and the Holy Spirit reside. But they reside not only on the earth. For floating above the three staffs, lighter and heavenly coloured, is another wooden staff of the same length. This is but one, for only Christians need a trinity to create an image of God in their minds. The Spirit of God moved upon the face of the waters, and

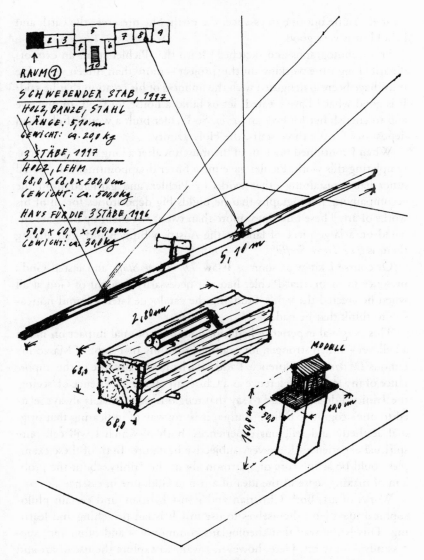

Figure 1.1a. Walter Pichler, *The Three Staffs and Floating Staff*

created, triune but one in essence, the earth. She preserves the earth and
behold, it is very good.

From photographs and sketches I learn that Pichler spent an extraor-
dinarily long time working on this project – more than fifteen years. He
must have been so delighted with the holiness of his creation that he said:
It is good what I have created; let us build a house for God, to preserve
and to cherish her for ever and ever. So Pichler built a wonderfully plain
depository for the three staffs, the Holy Trinity.

When I continued my tour of the museum after a long time spent con-
templating this work, Pichler gave me a bitter disappointment. I entered
other halls containing other works by Pichler, and gathered from the
accompanying photographs that he builds big depositories for all of his
works of art. These buildings, more than twenty of them by now, are sit-
uated on a large piece of land in the Austrian Burgenland, and among
them is *The Three Staffs*[10].

Of course I knew as soon as I saw *The Three Staffs* and tasted God's
presence in them, that Pichler had not necessarily thought of God at all
when he created the work. Studying the catalogue later, I found no reason to think that he had.

This personal experience had a profound emotional impact on me as
a believer – much stronger, for example, than my first sight of Masaccio's
famous *De trinità* in Florence. I add "as a believer", because of the importance of my frame of reference as a Christian on my experience of 'seeing'
the Trinity. I do not intend to say that religious experience is always related to one's cognitive beliefs. Rather, it is my way of indicating that original aesthetic and religious experiences, both of which I will call pure
spiritual experiences[11], are very subjective in nature. Both of these examples could be at the core of a sermon about the Trinity, about the problem of making sense of the idea of a triune God, one in essence…

Works of art, both Christian and non-Christian, and certain philosophical ideas lend themselves to use in Christian preaching and learning. This is the way that theologians commonly – and often very successfully[12] – use art. Here, however, I want to explore the use of art and
aesthetic theory in a broader way. Here I will describe 'the art world' and

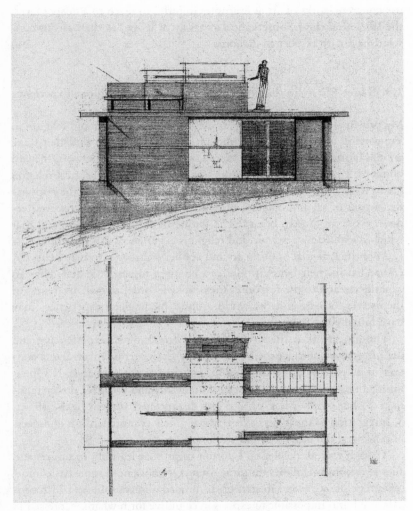

Figure 1.1b. *House for the Three Staffs*, 3rd Project, 1997
From: Walter Pichler, *Drawings: Sculptures: Buildings*,
Stedelijk Museum Amsterdam 1998; ISBN 3851270193

use concrete works of art as examples in order to reach to a deeper level: the level of aisthesis, observation as a way of living, as the basis of consciousness with respect to diakonia.

1.3. Three Phases in the Process of Aesthetic and Religious Experience

My principal concern, therefore, is with the relation of art and religion to 'enjoyment' and 'awareness of human suffering'. We will find that there are similarities and differences, as well as areas of overlap, between the two domains. I believe that the strongest similarity between art and religion lies in the nature of observing and experiencing, as well as in the response that works of art and religion, observed and experienced in creative freedom, evoke in human beings. The nature of this experiencing and that which is evoked by aesthetic and religious experiences can be similar[13].

My principal goal in using art and aesthetic theory is to help believers, embedded in their belief in God, to be open to aesthetic and religious experiences and to the responses they evoke in order to gain awareness of themselves, others, and the world around them. Such experiences may have moral connotations.

The process of aesthetic or religious observing and experiencing and the integration of this experience, whether it occurs in an academic context or as part of a learning group, consists of three phases: 1. Open-minded observation of an object (or an event) and intuitive understanding. 2. The (more or less) critical and distanciated analysis of the object. 3. Integration of the analysis to arrive at a new comprehension of aspects of ourselves, the other and the world[14].

Though I speak of phases, I do not mean that learning to understand an artwork always follows the same route. Often we need some basic information before we even can start open-minded observation. As Tillich says, "Although it is impossible to express in cognitive form what is expressed in artistic form, it is possible and often necessary to be guided by concepts to the point where concepts can be dismissed and immediate participation in the work of art can begin"[15]. So the phases can be interwoven, which is surely the case with (post-) modern readymades, as we will see below. Let us look at each of these three phases in greater detail.

Phase 1, Intuitive understanding: One observation, many possible ways of experiencing

Observation of reality can take place in several ways. Experiences in phase 1 consist of intuitive understanding through conscious, but nevertheless non-intentional open-minded and free observation.

Every experience, including religious, is made up of two components. These components are visible in German and Dutch, for we have two words for the one English word experience. The first is "Erlebnis" or "beleving", and second "Erfahrung" or "ervaring". So the first component is the "Erlebnis". Seeing the Unseen requires opening one's mind, an act of open and free receptivity – free of the opinions others would impose, and as free as possible from one's own prejudices. Only when these conditions of open and free receptivity are fulfilled can one observe in the way that seeing the Unseen requires.

The second component of experience is the "Erfahrung", the assimilation of that which has been observed. This requires creativity, or imagination. We know from social psychology but also from our own common sense that an observation only becomes an experience when it is cognitively and emotionally coloured by and incorporated into our frame of reference. That frame is the means by which we orient ourselves in everyday life, and it is shaped by our inherent nature, our life story, and our contemporary lifeworld and perception of it.

A good example of what happens when we observe is Ellen Harvey's *Seeing Is Believing*[16]. A video projection shows the painting process in real time. Harvey makes the viewer both the magician and the observer in the perception of work's illusionist space, for the left part of the video screen shows a photograph of a room, while the right part is a video of Harvey's hand painting a picture of the right part of the room. Harvey works very carefully, an observer cannot simply see the border between the photo and the painting. Like a magician, the viewer's eye makes a complete room out of the two parts, fitting them together within his internal frame of reference. The close observer, however, will also see that the left part is a still of half a real existing room, while only the right part is changing, is being painted, and this observation reveals the illusion in Harvey's work.

Thus on the one hand open-minded observation is coloured by our frame of reference, while on the other hand the observation affects us and our frame of reference in ways that cannot be described in purely logical terms.

The two steps of reception and imagination together make an experience. The open and free reception of a phenomenon enables a person subsequently to contemplate the Invisible in a creative manner entirely suited to her own personality and life context. This I call a 'spiritual experience'. My first encounter with Pichler's *The Three Staffs* is an example of the first phase of spiritual, intuitive and open-minded observation. My immediate response was based on my own frame of reference, for it would not necessarily have occurred to either the artist or other viewers to think of the Trinity when looking at the work. Conscious but nonintentional observation, combined with my frame of reference – a strong interest in architecture and theology, and my own pious disposition – resulted in my being profoundly affected by the work in both an aesthetic and a religious sense, although the response might have been purely aesthetic in one person and purely religious in another.

The most interesting similitude between art and religion, in my opinion, is the emotional response produced during the first, intuitive and open-minded observation; in this original emotional response aesthetic and religious observation are identical. It is in phase 2 that differences often become evident.

Phase 2, critical analysis: The (more or less) critical and distanciated analysis of the object

There are situations in which even a 'naive' observer will approach a work of art almost immediately from the second phase, that of critical analysis, and in which open-minded observation comes into play very little, if at all. With a tour group I visited the church of Santa Maria Novella in Florence, where an art historian explained to us Masaccio's famous fresco *De trinità,* the Holy Trinity, dating from 1427 (figure 1.2). We learned that this work represents the first time the theory of perspective was applied. Our attention was drawn to the powerful aura of God the Father, embracing his crucified Son, and to the curious little dove between them, representing the Holy Spirit. Typical colour combinations were pointed out. Gradually even group members unfamiliar with art were able to appreciate the content and significance of the fresco.

Ultimately, of course, there remained great individual differences in how the work was received. Reactions ranged from "Did you hear what she said about the colours, the perspective? This is real art! I'm glad I saw it with my own eyes!" to "What an intensely feeling artist, I can sense his insight into God's most profound mystery, the Holy Trinity!". In the latter case the critical insight is accompanied by emotional appreciation, as in phase 1; though in a more superficial and indirect form.

These examples illustrate the difference between the open-minded observation of phase 1 and the more analytical observation and judgement of phase 2. In both phases the aesthetic and, where applicable, religious experience will vary from one individual to another. The variation has to do with our frame of reference. When we observe, we discriminate. We see, hear, sense certain things, while not seeing, hearing, sensing others. Every observation, 'aisthesis', at the same time implies 'anaisthesis', as Welsch has pointed out.[17] This phenomenon of anaesthesia is consciously used by advertising. It is also used by many artists, such as Francis Bacon and Ann Grifalconi. They revise well-known works of art in such a way that the anaesthetic, hidden side of the original paintings is revealed[18]. The idea of anaesthesia is necessary to explain why we ask "Dare we observe?"

When one begins with an analytical approach it is very difficult to return to, let alone evoke directly, the original spiritual experience. That is why it is important to begin with phase 1, before moving on to the important task of analysing a work of art.

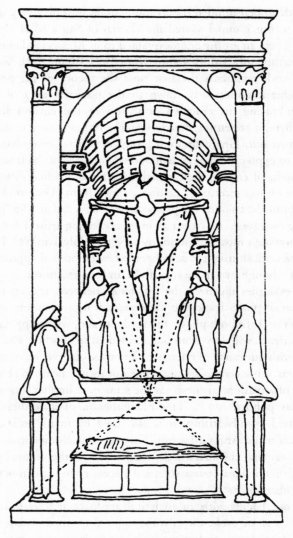

Figure 1.2 Masaccio, *De trinità*, about 1425. Fresc, 667 x 317 cm.
Florence, Santa Maria Novella.

Phase 1 and 2 again: The material side of art; the development of art and philosophy of art in the last two centuries

Until now I have spoken in a rather formal way about the two phases of observing and experiencing objects of art. We now turn to the content, or the material nature, of the objects. To understand the content of art, we need to ask: What is art, what is a work of art, that can be experienced aesthetically and perhaps even religiously? How will such an art experience be explained by theologians? For in the last two centuries aesthetics and theology have grown completely apart from each other, as we can see when we look at the development of art and aesthetics since Kant and Hume. In the following I will give a very brief overview of this historical development.

Since the beginning of the Enlightenment, artists have increasingly grown away not only from traditional religieus belief and traditional theology, but also from the traditional representational manner of painting, what is known in the visual arts as mimesis, the imitation of natural reality. Furthermore, especially since World War II, art in many cases has drifted away from the intentional search for beauty in either concrete or abstract forms and contents.

Visual artists like the American Jackson Pollock and the Dutchman Karel Appel, composers like the French Eric Satie, at a certain stage of their artistic careers abandoned preconceived plans to represent something, be it concretely or abstractly. 'Pop artists' like Andy Warhol and Bruce Naumann rejected traditional techniques and used subject matter drawn from the banality of urban America as the basis for their works. Sometimes their work, like the photographss of Cindy Sherman and the sculptures of Louise Bourgeois, acquires extra power from the hidden philosophical message. Today we live in a time, often called 'postmodern', in which everything is allowed, and every artist has his own style. Many artists opt for the banal, offering kitsch as art. What is art? What is a work of art?

Postmodern artists simply worked, creating with paint or sound, and left it to critics of art to decide whether these creations were in fact art and how they should be judged in terms of form, content, beauty and the like. In philosophy this led to new ways of judging art, and indeed philosophers like the Americans George Dickie Dickie and Arthur Danto, the Frenchwoman Anne Cauquelin and the Germans Martin Seel and Wolfgang Welsch, felt called on to determine what is or is not art. Dickie developed an approach to judging art that did not say whether a work is beautiful or not. He introduced a definition of a work of art, which does not depend on such subjective evaluations of aesthetic qualities of a work, but on the "instrumental goodness" of a work of art. "A work of art can produce valuable experiences"[19]. The problem, however, is: what kind of experiences are 'valuable experiences'; who establishes the intersubjective criteria to which something is judged to be art? Dickie mentions aesthetic qualities like unity, elegance, intensity and complexity of a work of art. Unity means, that a work of art exhibits coherence. Elegance means, that a work shows up refinement, and is well decorated. Intensity means, that a work of art has a powerful aura. Complexity means, that a work of art is not univocal, but consists of many elements. The more valuable properties a work of art is judged to possess, the more excellent it is. It is impossible to evaluate a work of art on strong aesthetical grounds, for these are never 'desinterested', but always stand in relation to the viewer's frame of reference.

An approach like Dickie's was urgently needed as more and more artists produced highly unconventional work. Those of us who visit art exhibitions often ask ourselves: "Why is this rubbish called art?"

In this confusion Dickie's approach to evaluating art creates some order. His method of judging art is part of what we have called 'phase 2', the analysis of art. In judging art on other than formal grounds one always runs the risk of basing the judgement on personal feelings, as I did with Pichler's The Three Staffs.

Is there a middle course between the emotional response to art and the formal theory of Dickie? Surely it must be possible to say more about the material nature of the experience of art than Dickie suggests. Dickie rules out every subjective criteria for determining whether something is 'art' because he fears that we will fall back into personal judgements.

Other philosophers of art, however, state that the judgement of a work of art always remains a matter of personal taste and prejudice both on the part of the artist and on the part of the critic. Characteristic of a work of art is that it is embedded in a context. From this context it takes on a moral and sometimes even a religious aura, which they refer to as the "world-transforming" ("weltbildende") significance of the work. Furthermore, not all artists simply create without thought for the meaning of what they are doing. Unlike Pollock, for example, some artists do have an idea of beauty or even some philosophical or moral idea in mind when they create. This is true to some extent of the Pop artists, and is by definition true of artists who aim to make some kind of social statement, often inspired by neo-marxism, feminism or religion. This kind of art is a "continuing reflective encounter with the world in which the work, far from being the end point of that process, acts as an initiator of and focus for the subsequent investigation of meaning"[20]. Grasping that meaning is the work of phase 3: comprehension, we discuss below. First, I introduce another influential American critic, Arthur Danto, who takes another approach to understanding art in phase 2.

Danto became well known for his book about contemporary art, *The Transfiguration of the Commonplace*[21] in 1981. A commonplace object, such as a Brillo soap box, becomes a work of art when Andy Warhol produces an exact imitation of it, with photographs on plywood. Warhol penetrated the institutionally recognized art world because his representations of ordinary objects evoked another world, creating in the viewer the shock of seeing something entirely new that transcended, or transfigured, the commonplace. As a result, it seems to be no longer possible to group the multiple forms of postmodern art in the same class as art from Giotto to Pollock; if we see art as "works of art", one work can be so different from another that we can only question its "family resemblance"[22] Therefore, the way a work of art was judged also changed the definition of art. In Danto's vision, "the being of a work of art is its meaning. Art is a mode of thought..."[23].

As a historian Danto concurs with Hegel's vision that a concept of art is finite, and is not a continuing story[24]. The idea of things being 'art' did

not originate until the 18th century, and perhaps we can make a historical distinction between art before Giotto (12th C.), art from Giotto to
Pollock (1960), and art in our time, "when anything can be a work of
art... Contemporary art celebrates the thought projected by the work,
which may itself have little distinction, aesthetically speaking"[25]. "So
what does it take to be an artwork in what I term Post-History?", Danto
wonders. He gives some examples, and the criterion "has nothing to do
with its maker merely declaring it to be art." Its being art, Danto declares,
is "implicated in its conceptual complexity, its purpose, and its means"[26].

Danto's premise appears to be that anything can be art, but that art
critics will judge the complexity of the concept, the degree of congru-
ence between the purpose of the concept and the work itself, and the
appropriateness of the means[27]. As an example, he points to the painters
Komar and Melamid, who had fled the Sowjet Union and ridiculed the
Soviet realism style in their work. After 1989, however, they had to look
for a new idea. They researched what the average American wanted in a
painting and, based on the results, made a painting called *Most Wanted
Painting*. Since 44% of Americans they surveyed thought blue was the
most beautiful colour, 44% of the painting is blue. The average
American also liked pictures of statesmen, happy families, and certain
animals, and all those things are in the painting. Of course, Danto
argues, this work is not art in itself, it does not have a place in the artworld as a painting. But as a "performance piece", consisting of the survey, the painting and all the surrounding publicity, it surely can be considered part of the artworld[28]. This example fits Danto's most recent definition. At the same time, however, Duchamps' readymades, which
Duchamp himself never considered to be art, but rather as a joke about
contemporary art around 1913 – and even Warhol's Brillo Box apparently do not meet Danto's criteria, even though they remain favourites
of his. How can one explain this?

In his most recent account of the Brillo Box story, Danto acknowl-
edges that since 1981 he had to change his mind about how we can judge
whether an object is a work of art. Now, he distinguishes three versions:
the 'real' Brillo box, designed in 1964 by a fine artist, Steve Harvey, who

"deserved a prize"[29]; Warhol's replica of the box from 1968, *Brillo Box*, and eighty-five Brillo boxes by the appropriationist artist Mike Bidlo, entitled *Not Andy Warhol*, in 1991[30]. The differences between the works are invisible. What makes a something art is not something that meets the eye, but rather its "meaning, which is the task of art criticism to make explicit: The definition of art remains a philosophical problem." Anything can be proclaimed a work of art, provided that a "suitable art criticism" is invented for it.[31]

Even in 2000, Danto's theory is not, in my opinion, conclusive[32]. The end of art (in one way) is not the end of art (in another way). While Danto claims that his theory corresponds to Hegel's, it does not. The absolute Spirit is beyond religion and art. It remains unclear to me what contemporary art really is. As said above, some of Duchamps' and Warhol's most intriguing works do not correspond to Danto's definition, although even Danto admits – and many would agree – that they are indeed works of art.

Perhaps Danto is too much a modern analytical philosopher to accept what he himself says: that everything can be a work of art. Ultimately, though theoretically not convincing, Danto's work, especially his ideas about metaphorical thinking, the transfiguration of the commonplace, and his religious idea that an ordinary human person is God[33], are both compelling and useful. He writes about what is 'in the air', about the coherence between art, culture and everyday life, and implies that only that which falls into this coherence is art.

Danto would be very critical of my experiential concept of art and religion. He does not acknowledge anything like what I call 'phase 1', or intuitive understanding, for his only focus is on things that "the eye cannot see".[34]

Yet, in my opinion, phase 1 is indispensable. I walk through a museum and see an ordinary object, like the Brillo box. According to Danto I would need to know more about it to decide whether it is a work of art. But ordinary things can also be enlightening in and of themselves. Look at nature. Look at the titles I gave to photographs I made, walking around Princeton after being snowed in for four days: "The New York

Times, 1/18/2002, waiting to be read after thaw"; "The dismissal of the Cross: cyclist xing". Even without prior knowledge, we can learn much simply by looking at what is in front of us, and this is true of art before 1960 as well as of contemporary art. Though clearly some works lend themselves better to 'contemplation' than others.

Phase 3: Comprehension

Comparing phase 1 of intuitive understanding with Dickie's vision, we cannot help but conclude that he has little interest in phase 1. Dickie's method completely ignores the emotional and existential aspects that for most people are precisely what art and religion are all about: the evocation of feelings of beauty, cruelty, anger, injustice. These emotions in a sense prepare people for action: weeping, acquiring strength to give aid or offer resistance, and so on.

Therefore we need to look beyond phase 2 to the significance of aesthetic and religious experiences in and their benefit for everyday life. This is the work of phase 3, where feedback to phase 1 takes place. This method of bridging of subjective observations, theoretical distanciated perspectives and personal comprehension of a fragment of the life-world, Wolfgang Welsch calls "transversality"[35]. Transversality is transversal reason, i.e. thinking in pluralities, which goes hand in hand with making connections; thinking in heterogenity and interweaving disparate elements; or thinking in plurality and transition together. The concept of transversality is a useful one for aesthetics, as well for an open-minded view of Christian religion as a base for fruitful plurality, even if we have always in mind the material source, namely the Bible and Christian tradition.

Welsch and Cauquelin also propose steps that are similar to the ones I described[36]. For example, Cauquelin's statement that the judgment of a work of art ends with its theoretical, moral or subjective discourse in the lifeworld corresponds to phase 3. We have described phase 3 as 'integration of the analysis to arrive at a new comprehension of aspects of ourselves, the other and the world'. So now we turn to the comprehension of spiritual, aesthetic or religious experiences as part of the lifeworld. And we find that art and religion have much in common.

1.4. Transcendence in and Transfiguration by Art and Religion

Distinct cultural phenomena such as art and religion overlap. The American philosopher of art Arthur Danto has perhaps expressed this most succinctly in the title of his book we discussed before, The Transfiguration of the Commonplace. Warhol's imitation of a Brillo box transcends, or transfigures, the common soap box. This kind of transcendence can be called religious, but it is not religious in the sense that I describe religion[37], nor is it ethical in the general sense of the word. As pointed out above, Danto's "meaning" transcends the commonplace, but he avoids ascribing religious or ethical meaning to a work, even where it would be possible, as seen in the following example.

In 1998 I visited the P.S.1 Contemporary Art Center in New York. This is a place where young artists have a chance to show their work in huge halls, exhibiting it as they believe it should be seen. The museum asks famous art critics, like Arthur Danto, to comment on the works, and these comments are displayed next to the works. One of the artists whose work was on display at the P.S.1 Contemporary Art Center who intrigued me was Lynne Yamamoto (figure 1.3).

On a white wall the viewer sees about 200 thick spikes about 3 inches long, sticking out of a horizontal beam of about 5 yards. On the tip of each spike is a white sticker bearing a short, handwritten word such as 'wash', 'dry', 'care', 'clean', 'cook', 'bake' – words generally associated with the household – but interrupted every seven words by a word such as 'pain', 'try', 'love', 'hope', or 'birth'.

In his comments on Yamamoto's work Arthur Danto wrote, "I like this work very much. Especially the long dark shadows of the spikes on the white wall, made by the spots." While I agree with Danto's observation, I felt that there was much more to this installation. To me there was

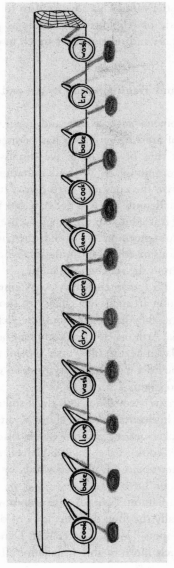

Figure 1.3 Lynne Yamamoto, *Untitled*, P.S.1 Contempory Art Center, New York 1998 (impression of the author; fragment)

strong contrast between the monotony of the words on the spikes, the sense of being nailed to one's situation, and the glimpses of another, more existential experience, the breaking through of 'pain', 'try', 'love', 'hope', 'birth'. I do not understand why a critic like Danto would not see or comment on this aspect. A matter of anaesthesia? Perhaps, like Dickie, he wants to avoid making a judgement about the moral and existential aspects of a work of art.

A recent installation of Yamamoto, *Resplendent*, is, as the title promises, much more beautiful, and still the moral connotation is obvious. The New York Times critic Ken Johnson describes it as a "delicately theatrical, symbolically complex meditation on war, death and beauty. Each of nine massive, clear-glass bell jars shaped like bombs is engraved with a cherry blossom sign that once decorated a World War II Japanese fighter plane. On the walls, pink cut-paper cherry blossoms pinned like butterflies seem to drift down to pile up near the floor. At the center of most blossoms is the face of a Japanese soldier who was killed in the war." The room is about nine by four yards, with one almost open side. The combination of the dreamy, spring-like atmosphere and the hidden power of war is both fantastic and awful.

I myself feel at home with artists like Yamamoto, whose work expresses something like the "transcendence of common beliefs". Behind the immanent commonplace, which is usually not difficult to express, as Danto shows, there is more: the invisible. To express this demands a different kind of creative act: art as the revelation of the invisible, as Paul Klee said. And this takes us right into the middle of the broad, hazy area between art and religion. If we want to use the term 'transcendence' in a theological sense, we must be clear that it concerns the transition from the immanent to the unconditional nature of the ultimate.

Practical theologian Horst Schwebel of the University of Marburg distinguishes three kinds of transcendence in art. I propose to add three more, two of which are based on the types suggested by Tillich, whose classification also forms the basis of Schwebel's three types.[38]

The first is transcendence as the ecstatic experience of a breakthrough, as suggested by Tillich. If a work of art is expressive in its style, the religious content of the work can break open existing reality. Tillich mentions Van Gogh's *Hills at St. Remy*, and Munch's *The Scream*.

Second, there is transcendence as mystical experience, as being freed from the world or "Entweltlichung". This we find in the work of Kandinsky. He wrote about this in his early study entitled *About the Spiritual in Art*. Mondriaan spent his whole life seeking to make the perfect painting of ultimate mystical experience. After World War II we find the search for the mystical in the work of artists like Barnett Newman, Mark Rothko and Yves Klein.

Third, there is transcendence as sacramental experience, as the presence of the holy within our reality. An outstanding example of this attitude is Joseph Beuys' idea of *Every man a Christ*. Other artists working in this direction, notes Schwebel, try to pinpoint the "sakramental EST in the reality of life".

The fourth kind of transcendence is the religious-humanistic experience of the better world, sometimes too idealistically foreseen in our time. Tillich refers to works of Poussin and Ingres to illustrate this kind of transcendence.

A fifth type of transcendence, one that is of great importance to the present study, is transcendence as prophetic-critical experience, warning that holiness without justice must be rejected. Tillich points to Goya's *Que Valor*! (What Courage!), and many of the installations discussed in Chapter 5 fall into this category.

The sixth and last type is related to the first, but in my opinion different: Transcendence of common reality or beliefs, "of the commonplace" (Danto uses the phrase about Warhol; it could be applied to Nauman too), but also the shifts between the experience of the real and our projections, fantasies and desires, as shown by Janet Cardiff, who will be discussed further on.

What strikes us in all six kinds of transcendence is how little they have in common with Dickie's criteria for evaluating art. His type of analysis is only one of the possible approaches in phase 2. Moreover, we consider analysis to be only one of the three phases of the process of aesthetic experience. The account of the different kinds of transcendence in art has much more to do with the third phase, that of grasping the significance

("Sinn") of art in our life, as a way of comprehending ourselves, the other and the world in a philosophical, moral and religious way.

Important in Tillich's account of the comprehension of art is that we will never fully grasp the significance of a work of art if we use only language. Verbal conceptualization and linguistic evaluation is only one aspect of the philosophy of art and only one aspect of a theology of art as well. There is always a residue of meaning which cannot be interpreted except on the level of emotions, or bodily perceptions and, not least, by way of action. For instance, if we enter Janet Cardiff's *To Touch*, a room where we have to touch a wooden table to become part of an audiovisual artwork.

Connotations other than aesthetic and religious ones come into play when we go beyond strict analysis, both in discussions and in our feelings and actions. All of the material attributes we encounter in aesthetic experiences, everything we can determine cognitively about a work of art we seek to accommodate within our frame of reference. But there is more going on. We interweave a plurality of perspectives in a transversal way. We look for connections between the things we already feel, know and remember, our existing subjective, moral and theoretical standpoints on the one hand, and our new experiences on the other. When the object of our observation is modern art, these connections are usually not self-evident. We often need to appeal to our imaginative powers. For in modern art one has to abstract from concrete reality. Art then becomes a transfiguration of everyday life, a metaphor.

Thus we cannot understand, or comprehend, everything about a work of art. According to Welsch we try to bridge gaps between facts and feelings, but there will also remain 'zones of intangibility' ("Zonen des Unfaßlichen")[39].

And does not the same apply to religion in modern times? The reality of living with God too can no longer be presented as either a natural or a metaphysical reality, but is accessible only through the suspension of logical-rational thought, i.e. as a metaphor. A believer would say: as a metaphor of the transcendent reality of God.

Many works of art have a highly metaphorical and even transcendent character, as does religious work, and it is evident from these works that the

modern metaphors hidden in art and religion can refer back to the immanent origin in everyday life. Christians see in the person of Jesus a metaphor
for the everyday figure of God (Jüngel). So today aesthetic as well as
religious experiences may be world-transforming, in a moral sense. Such
experiences point upwards, but are located in the middle of everyday life.

In phase 3, the phase of comprehension in everday life situations, we
grasp the meaning of a work of art for our own lives. This meaning may
be either "l'art pour l'art", "contemplation for the sake of contemplation", and fixed on pure enjoyment, or it may be world-transforming, but
in any case it is always mixed with other kinds of experience. Dickie is
right in saying that it is impossible to judge aesthetic quality as such. But
we are not content with Dickie's approach. We accept an analytical judgement, as phase two, but want another step, to discover the personal, existential, religious and moral implications of – some – works of art. The
observer's frame of reference plays a crucial role in shaping the subjective
experience of a work of art. We use, next to a theoretical-cognitive disposition, the competence of 'transversal reason' and bodily skills[40] to
comprehend the meaning of an artwork for our personal lifeworld.

We have now seen that philosophers of art like the American George
Dickie make use only of phase 2 to interpret a work of art. The encounter
with Masaccio's De trinità is another example of phase 2. Applications of
art, books about and guides to particular works of art also are based, of
necessity, on phase 2. While many committed colleagues start, like
Dickie, from phase 2, but also include some ind of phase 3, I hold that
we should not dispense with phase 1, even when working in an academic sense. My description of Pichler's work began with phase 1 and ended
temporarily in phase 2; I will return to it now.

1.5. Conclusion: Pichler's *The Three Staffs*, in Three Phases

What happens when I look back at Pichler's work in a more open-minded way in relation to the opinions of others, that is, somewhat more in
the sense of "neither disinterested, nor purely subjective", but thinking in
a transversal way?

The first phase, that of intuitive understanding, remains the same. My own preconceptions led me to respond to *The Three Staffs* with awe, a kind of "frui deo", as Augustine called it, or enjoyment of God. As a believer I tasted in this work a symbol of the triune God, even though I was aware that Pichler presumably did not have the Trinity in mind. Such a subjective experience, coloured by one's own frame of reference, is legitimate, but it can generally be shared with others only by means of non-verbal communication or metaphoric language. So I could perhaps use this experience in a sermon. Generally, though, it has no direct significance for others.

What about the second phase, the phase of analysis? Following the analytical approach proposed by Dickie, one might come up with the following syllogisms that would end with the conclusion that Pichler's work is indeed good art:

Unity in a work of art is always valuable. *The Three Staffs* is unified. Therefore *The Three Staffs* is valuable, that is, has some degree of good in it.

Intensity, the aura emanating from a work of art, is always valuable. This work, *The Three Staffs*, has intensity. Therefore *The Three Staffs* is valuable, that is, has some degree of good in it.

Dickie would regard *The Three Staffs* as a work of art, but his judgment would be based on a limited range of criteria[41]. Public appreciation of Pichler's work would, I believe, be similarly limited; only a small group will warm to his ideas about art.

In the catalogue, neither Pichler himself nor Rudi Fuchs, the organizer of the exhibition[42], say anything about the meaning of the works. Fuchs follows the line of the artist in stressing the use of traditional craftmanship and his controlled, even obsessive, symmetrical order, which is rare in visual art. Symmetry is used to bring about a motionless and concentrated fixation of form and contour. Craftmanship, order, the use of light, all contribute to the contemplation of the work. Pichler shuns the expressive, refuses the narrative.

The third phase is comprehension of meaning for everyday life, understanding renewed by analysis, with all senses. In my intuitive understanding of *The Three Staffs*, the three wooden staffs represented the Trinity. Upon analysis I know that my intuition is acceptable only if the Trinity of my imagination is the "immanent" Trinity – God resting in herself – and not the so-called "economic Trinity"[43]. From my own experience I know that *The Three Staffs* did not agitate me, did not make me eager to go back to work, and after analysing the work I understand why this is so.

Consequently, Pichler's artwork could be classified as type six, 'transcendence of common reality'. For I am well aware that quite possibly no one else will ever think about the Trinity when looking at this work. As Rudi Fuchs notes, Pichler more than any other sculptor is concerned with symmetry. Fuchs concludes that this silent, endless search for symmetry suggests longing. It represents that which is not to be found outside Pichler's property in Burgenland: As it is here, so it is good. Be quiet, stay with the things your hand finds to do, and it will become good.

Whether this experience of modest, quiet longing for the whole can be interpreted only in an aesthetic or also in a religious way is the prerogative first and foremost of the artist-creator, but also of the viewer, the person observing the work of art as a free and autonomous subject. There is and will always be a difference between immanent spiritual experiences that anybody can have, and immanent spiritual experiences that believers have when they interpret a particular experience as religious, because it is accompanied by the feeling that God is part of the experience.

To some extent this difference, this gap can be bridged when we use our possibilities of transversal reason and shared bodily skills.

But in another way this gap between the profane and the sacral has always existed, as a 'zone of intangibility' ("Zone des Unfaßlichen"), and the task of enlightened human beings is to learn to live it consciously.

CHAPTER 2.

LONGING
The Spiritual Basis of Certain Aesthetic and Religious Experiences

2.1. A Spiritual Teaching-Learning Process

Longing

Spirituality is a diffuse notion. Why do we call somebody we meet almost at first glance a 'spiritual person'? Why do many people seem to exhibit almost no sign of spirituality? What are signs of spirituality and what is the outcome of a spiritual attitude? In my view, spirituality is a universal mental capacity, though one that sometimes remains largely undeveloped.

The American anthropologist Roy Rappaport, in his posthumously published book, *Ritual and Religion in the Making of Humanity*[1], starts with a thought that he repeats very often, which is that humanity "is a species that lives, and can only live, in terms of meaning it must construct in a world devoid of intrinsic meaning but subject to physical law". This search for meaning as a mental possibility is what differentiates human beings from other living species. Humans distinguish the physical and the meaningful. With their unbridled consciousness they can imagine things they cannot perceive. Their capacities of imagination and spiritual feelings are grounded in innate basic needs, often unconscious, which are shaped in the first years of life. In other words, the wish to satisfy some kind of basic need will be awakened, or not, in a form strongly determined by personal nature, socialization, biography, the context of life, and the culture as a whole. The same is true of the mental capacity for spirituality.

What does spirituality bring to the development of a person's frame of reference and search for meaning? In many religions or world views and

in aesthetics there are images in which cultural manifestation is spiritually coloured. I call these images spiritual, because they have world-creat-
ing potential[2]. They set up the spiritual dynamic that comforts us in our
suffering, that is the source of enjoyment and that incites us to action,
although for action to occur other components are also indispensible,
such as the will[3].

Here I do not want to give an absolute, but rather a personal definition of spirituality that can be used as a contemporary, secular, Western
pedagogical-didactical concept, as well as in a Christian context. In our
handbook *De gemeente en haar verlangen* I use the concept of spirituality
as "verlangen", longing – longing for the righteous and good life, for the
Kingdom of God – as the basis of Christian hope.

In this case spirituality has a religious content. However, spirituality
also has a secular content and to me it is interesting to maintain this secular basis[4]. This definition of spirituality can be used in the field of ethics,
art and religion. It implies that the material and the immaterial are of
equal value. It is also clearly a product of the Enlightenment, for it is for-
mulated in general terms and is not bound to a particular society or religion. My definition is as follows:

*Spirituality is the strength of mind, which we call longing, of people offer-
ing resistance to suffering:* longing not yet expressed and dynamic; longing
for insight into the *origin* of life; longing for insight into self, others and
the world around us; and longing for safety, justice, love, beauty and
enjoyment in the *present*; longing for fulfilment in the *future*.

Spirituality, in the sense of longing, is not to be understood as an
equivalent of aesthetics or religion. It is, rather, one of the qualities that
lend a special colour to aesthetics, religion and world view. It is a human
mental possibility. Since it exists only in expression, it must be given
expression through the materials of art and world view, in sensory content like words, sounds, smells and images. In those expressions we discover the five possible outcomes of spiritual processes: they provoke won-
der (1), they give enjoyment (2), they lead to ritual actions (3) which
serve as a source of strength in life's suffering and turmoil (4), and they
inspire just and good actions (5).

So, spirituality has to do with religious and philosophical accounts of suffering, longing and hope. In the International Journal of Children's Spirituality, it is assumed that children, often at a very young age, present a clearly observable spirituality in everyday life. These primal spiritual feelings, linked to basic needs, can be seen as the starting point for development that leads to 'primal faith', the permanent foundation needed for a developed belief system, religious or not, in children, young people and adults.

Zadkine: De verwoeste stad (The Destruction of Rotterdam)

I conclude this section with an example of aesthetic spirituality. In Rotterdam, on the banks of the Maas River, stands a famous monument by Ossip Zadkine (figure 2.1). It depicts a man without a heart, who has been ripped apart by pain, despair, rage and bewilderment at the demonic violence that human beings inflict upon one another. What is spiritual in this sculpture[5]?

First, it is, in Rappaport's words, imaginative rather than realistic, since rationally we know that a human being cannot exist without a heart. Second, it expresses what is not true in a discursive way: it depicts a person, but stands for a city, a city full of people whose heart has been destroyed. Third, it is dynamic: it awakens forces of resistance against demonic powers in mankind.

The image depicts suffering and evokes spiritual longings for insight: How could humanity come to this (in the past)? At the same time it evokes a yearning for justice and for good (now), desires that drive people to take dynamic action (for a better future).

What is peculiar about this interpretation of the spiritual aspects of Zadkine's sculpture is that it can only be arrived at with the help of rational knowledge. The viewer must know what happened to Rotterdam during World War II, and must know something about the functioning of the human body. The figure also appeals to pre-existing knowledge of the horrors of Nazism. Thus Zadkine's sculpture illustrates how spirituality,

Figure 2.1a Ossip Zadkine, *De verwoeste stad*
(The Destruction of Rotterdam)

Figure 2.1b Ossip Zadkine, *De verwoeste stad*
(The Destruction of Rotterdam)

the hidden 'longing' that is present in every human being, comes to consciousness when three conditions are met: 1. The spiritual must be present in a material form, for example in words or, in the case of Zadkine's monument, a bronze figure. 2. The spiritual must tie in with already existing feelings and, in most cases, with pre-existing knowledge as well. 3. The spiritual must be conveyed in such a way that it can lead to enjoyment, to words, song or dance, and to just and good actions.

A paradox

The co-existence of physical and the spiritual meaning, the interpretation of works of art and of religious metaphors with their hidden, one might say virgin, spirituality, creates a paradox. On the one hand spirituality, when not interpreted in words or images, remains something personal and internal to each individual, something that is not perceived by others, though when it is expressed, it turns out that people can help each other develop the hidden spirituality that they carry within themselves. On the other hand rites and symbols and art have a spiritual, dynamic effect only when they do not need to be interpreted, in other words when the spiritual is still 'almost hidden', when one is receptive to it solely by virtue of what is already present in one's own consciousness. This paradox of the spiritual is the reason that many works of art and religious rituals that are repetitions of already well-worn ideas or that require excessive encoding, lose their spiritual function. As we saw above, too much critical analysis (phase 2) in any of the six aesthetic styles is fatal for the revelation of transcendent meaning of an artwork.

2.2. Performances: Koelewijn's *Cleaning the Rietveld Pavilion*

Performances

In this section I propose to focus on the link between spirituality and performances in art and religion. The term 'performances' is used in a very broad sense as *any activity aimed at producing* installations as well as other kinds of sculptures, and at *preparing and executing* sacral or profane rituals and art performances per se. In Chapter 4, this definition will be used as the basis for a pedagogical method, and in Chapter 6 as a means of theological study of diakonia.

Cleaning the Rietveld Pavilion

The example of performance that I would like to discuss is a work of art, both installation and performance, by the Dutch artist Job Koelewijn, who now works in New York. In an essay on Koelewijn written by Carel Blotkamp[6], Blotkamp argues that the concept of the vernacular may provide us with a convenient approach to Koelewijn's art. For Koelewijn is a so-called postmodern performance artist, who rejects the modernist idea that there is a universal language of forms.

Koelewijn's first work, by which he sought and gained publicity, was a performance in the spring of 1992, after he had completed his studies at the Rietveld Art Academy in Amsterdam. It is entitled *Het schoonmaken van het Rietveld paviljoen* or "Cleaning the Rietveld Pavilion" (figure 2.2).

The performance consisted of four women, armed with cleaning equipment and ladders, spending an entire day rendering the school's small glass exhibition pavilion absolutely spotless.

Blotkamp writes, "While quite simple on the surface, the work contains a number of references which lend it more than one layer of meaning." It can be interpreted as a spring cleaning...in the figurative sense as well. For Koelewijn looks back on his years in the Rietveld Institute with mixed feelings and is now putting things to rights. The performance also recalls the ritualistic nature of cleaning house. In many religious rites a major role is reserved for the cleansing of the body, an object or an area (..), in order to make it receptive to the divine and – Koelewijn seems to be saying – to art.

"On another level, the work is a reference to Gerrit Rietveld, whose name the academy bears, and who designed the building which houses it.

Figure 2.2. Job Koelewijn, *Cleaning the Rietveld Pavilion*. Photo Koelewijn, from: *New Dutch Sculptors. Job Koelewijn*, published by New Sculpture Museum, Rijssen NL 1999, pp. 24f.

… Rietveld's architecture is regarded as typically Dutch, and for centuries Dutch cleanliness has been legendary. …But the most vernacular aspect of the performance – both visually and intrinsically – was the way [Koelewijn] succeeded in weaving his personal background into the work."

The women in the performance are Koelewijn's mother and three aunts, wearing the traditional costume of Spakenburg where Job Koelewijn was born (figure 2.3)

In the book Koelewijn devoted to his installation, he intersperses photographs of the installation with white pages containing brief statements, printed in blue, about sobriety and cleanliness, as well as famous texts like a quotation from the Spanish mystic Theresa of Avila: "A woman engaged in cleaning does not lose control over her senses". Here, Blotkamp writes,

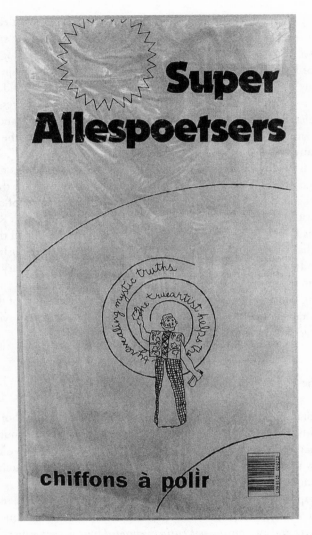

Figure 2.3. Job Koelewijn, Women in the traditional costume of Spakenburg.
Photo Koelewijn, from: *New Dutch Sculptors. Job Koelewijn*, published by
New Sculpture Museum, Rijssen NL 1999, p. 17

"everyday chores involved in the performance are elevated to an ethical or religious level". Blotkamp also notes, interestingly, that "strictly speaking, the text is not accessible to foreign readers, who would only recognize the names of Rietveld and Theresa of Avila, at most... But Koelewijn made a conscious decision to employ this vernacular, apparently confident that anyone not familiar with Dutch geography and traditional dress would nonetheless grasp the essence of the work: a Frenchman..." (and I add, anyone familiar with the work of Gauguin,) "...might think of the women of Brittany".

I recall the four aspects of the performance Blotkamp brings to mind. First, that of spring cleaning and, even more, being cleansed of the problems associated with his time at the academy. Second, the rite of cleaning away dust in order to be receptive to art. Third, a hommage to Rietveld, a famous Dutch architect. And fourth, the being cleansed of all the difficulties that Koelewijn had with his very traditional and religiously orthodox family and family life. This process of cleansing is necessary so that he can start out on his own, freely chosen artistic life.

Spring cleaning, the process of getting rid of the remnants of the dark winter that we want to be relieved of, is reminiscent of what I will call a basic need to start a new life, over and over again.

2.3. The Use of Rituals and Works of Art

As Blotkamp points out, Koelewijn's work is also a kind of ritual. Koelewijn is used as an example to introduce this section about rituals and other sacral or profane activities that can be adapted as didactical methods in the classroom and for adult education in the church. I will call them performances and installations. Often they are both.

Rappaport, in his book about ritual and religion, defines the term 'ritual' as denoting "the *performance* of more or less *invariant* sequences of *formal* acts and utterances *not entirely encoded* by the performers"[7]. This definition includes only the structure of ritual, and encompasses much more than religious behaviour, though Rappaport based it on tribal rites.

In themselves the four elements – italicized above – constituting the structure of ritual he proposes are not unique to ritual, but the relations among them are. The first element is self-evident: without performance there is no ritual. The last of the four elements mentioned means that a ritual is to some extent traditional, and was encoded in former times. A new ritual is always based on or composed of elements of existing ritual. Rituals do not just originate in the mind of the current performer, and it is this that principally differentiates them from other types of performances, like the ones we can use in school or church as didactical methods, although I will propose further on that our educational performances must have to do with primal, unconscious, human feelings and basic needs. A new ritual is always based on or composed from elements of existing rituals.

The second and third element are still more closely interrelated. If the liturgical order is invariant, a ritual is formal in two respects. First it is not a spontaneous happening. Second, a ritual is formal because it has no – direct – material effect on the way of living of the participants. Although emotions could arise which eventually lead to some kind of action in the life-world, principally rituals confirm conventions and seal social contracts that together construct the integrated conventional order[8].

Rappaport's agnostic vision of the nature of rituals is not essentially unlike those of Christian theologians like the German Werner Jetter, the American Ronald Grimes and the Dutchman Gerard Lukken[9]. Like Jetter, Rappaport stresses that a ritual connects people within a given order, while they can interpret it in their own way. This characteristic of ritual makes a performance useful as an educational method. Though each observer/participant interprets it according to his own frame of reference, the ritual unites people. This is an eminent point today. People construct their vision of the world's order, in part, socially and symbolically[10]. The more isolated and homogeneous a culture is, the more all members share the same norms and values. In fact, every culture needs a certain, ritually confirmed order. Today, however, the concept of 'order' is problematic. Rappaport impressively deconstructs the order of Christianity and Enlightenment, that brought us "diabolical lies" and the "homo economicus", a one-sided, empty humanity. But in the traditions of the primeval age of the Aboriginals and even in the basic truth of the "book religions", he argues, we can perhaps find a new dream.

Rappaport believes that we must stop lying about the biblical *shalom*. Shalom is not primarily meant as an otherworldly resting in peace, as a warning *memento mori*. Shalom is an integral part of *tsedaka*, righteousness, the all encompassing good order reflected in the Jewish narratives of Thora and Nebi-im. The first Christians, mostly Jews themselves, also did not believe that after death we would inhabit a heaven cut loose from earth, but rather in a new earth under new heavens, "wherein dwelleth Tsedaka" (2 Peter 3:13). This myth about the just and good life is also found in other cultures. Rappaport found it among the aboriginal Australians. In my opinion this myth, existing in various vernacular forms, is still the basic and unquestionable truth of created life. The myth of the just and good life can support people in their personal lives as they seek to meet their basic needs.

Our rituals and our didactic performances, profane as well as sacral, can use as their basis the myths about tsedaka, about bringing shalom to the whole of creation. But we have been warned now. Not only Rappaport, but every ritualist scholar, stresses the fundamental ambivalence of rituals. The same applies when teachers use performances and installations as a didactic method[11].

2.4. The Rule of Ritual, Performance and Installation

Why are people interested in ritual? As the foregoing suggested, participating in rituals and other performances often appeals to our five senses and to every mental ability. Participating in a ritual is quite different from hearing or reading something and assimilating it intellectually and emotionally. Even story-telling only uses our sense of hearing. Learning something by hearing or reading it helps satisfy our longing for insight into questions about our human existence. But people do not only want insight. We need to practice every sense, practice our mental capabilities like thinking, knowing and willing, and experience our spiritual and physical feelings.

People have, over and above the need for insight, many other basic needs, which also may have to do with religious and moral questions related to existential experiences of life. As Rappaport notes, a human being can reflect consciously on his situation of life and the many contingencies of existence, including social relations, suffering, death and ethical problems. People not only have the need for insight, but also for security, acknowledgment, trust and so on.

A ritual, and hence creating an installation or a performance, could work powerfully in one of the following six domains of basic experiences relating to basic needs and functions that have to do with religion and other philosophies of life[12]:

1. Experiencing the good (meaning of life; aesthetics; for religious people: the vision of God, Augustine's "frui deo", or: enjoying God and creation)
2. Human responsibility and failing (ethics, e.g. personal or ecological questions; for religious people: diaconate)
3. The finiteness of existence; coping with evil and suffering (contingency of existence);
4. Guidance in cases of anger, fear, aggression, mourning, stress and trauma (guidance of the life circle);
5. Insight into the meaning of life and the nature of the cosmos, and experiencing the tension between transcendence and corporality (cultural education);
6. Experience of community, social relations (community building; societal studies).

The creation of performances

What constitutes a performance? What is the process by which it occurs, and how does it 'work'? As an example, let us look at a particular kind of theatrical performance. When a comedian makes jokes, he attempts, by making people laugh, to cheer them up; his aim is merriment. The 'ritual' is the performance of 'making jokes', the method, or process, is 'to make people laugh by telling jokes'. Often this process of performance may be expressed in the passive, as in this case 'being made to laugh' is also an important part of what is going on in the ritual. When the comedian's performance is successful, in other words it achieves its aim, the outcome or effect of the ritual is merriment, and people feeling better.

Terms used:

P – the *ritual*: (or: the installation)	the performance of 'making jokes'
M – the *method*: (both form and expression)	the things done within the ritual by the performer: 'to make people laugh by telling jokes'
the passive process: (both: form and expression)	the things happening within the ritual with the audience: 'being made to laugh'
E – the *effect*: (impression)	the outcome or aim: 'merriment', 'feeling better'

When all these elements are put together, will the desired effect be achieved? Not necessarily. Obviously there are other aspects involved in a successful performance. For example the method 'making people laugh by telling jokes' demands a huge amount of preparation. A comedian often takes a year to create a new show and try it out.

Yet another aspect is the subjective response of the participants. The participants must feel good about the performance. The performance must match the subjective experience of the participants. Whether they can assimilate the performance and appreciate it will depend on their personal frame of reference: their opinions and beliefs, their tastes, and especially their state of mind at the time, for example whether they are happy, afraid, tired, insecure and so on.

Religious performances must match the emotions invoked by the religious narrative inherent in the performance. Religious as well as moral performances must address basic needs. In and through the performance we become part of the reality evoked by the performance. The power of ritual, and hence the power of performance, is to help us to feel integrated in a group without losing individual identity and to cope with libidinal and aggressive emotions[13].

The performance process has been extensively discussed in the philosophy of art of the past century. In Chapter 1 we have already made a short excursion into the philosophy of art, which is also useful for this chapter. Art is always 'aesthetic', meaning that it has to do with aisthesis, observing. But it is not a matter of beauty alone. Art can also have societal and moral meaning; it can inhabit 'world-transforming' ideas, and it can be a vehicle for the longing that is spirituality.

The form and content of a work of art determines the effect it has on participants and spectators, on what they observe and feel. But what about the process of creating a work of art or a performance? What about the observations and feelings of the artist, the teacher, the student? Is it simply a matter of following a prescribed method, of programming a computer, of putting streaks and dots of paint of various colours on canvas? Of course not. The artist has something in mind, he tries to give form to his ideas. Naturally, the nature of those ideas is more easily determined in the work of a seventeenth-century painter than in that of a modern abstract painter. But art today has new possibilities. In postmodern art everything is possible. Many works of art can be compared with rituals in many ways: they have an intended religious or moral meaning, and aim to produce a particular religious or moral effect.

In Chapter 1 I identified six kinds of transcendence in art. I will use one of these kinds, the transcendence of common reality or beliefs, as seen in Koelewijn's *Cleaning the Rietveld Pavilion*, as an example. This kind of transcendence is also seen in the shifts between the experience of common reality and our projections, fantasies and desires that are so vividly represented by Janet Cardiff. Her works, like every good work of art, express something by their form – the way the materials are or will be worked over and arranged – and they present, by their form and expression, something that represents a certain reality for the artist or for the participants and spectators. Consider *The Dark Pool* by Cardiff and her partner Miller (1995; figure 2.4). "On entering the doorway to *The Dark Pool*, one encounters a realm of suspended animation (...) deserted of occupants; it has been left to decay beneath ever-accumulating layers of dust and debris"[14]. "The group of makeshift tables is completely covered by objects: books, photos, bare speakers, wire, light bulbs, pages from crumbling notebooks, rocks, a typewriter, a well-travelled trunk with a miniature scene inside. The viewer moves through the piece, triggering snippets of sound: an overheard conversation, a woman telling a story, a piano playing, unidentifiable noices, a portion of a movie soundtrack. This dark installation plays with its disjointed narrative, exploring how we construct our realities through fact and fantasy" (Cardiff). Cardiff and Miller wanted to create an environment that removed the visitor from the art gallery into some abandoned place where sounds and objects stir up dusty memories of an everchanging life story, once the narrative of the occupants who have mysteriously disappeared, now the multiple narratives of the visitors. "We wanted The Dark Pool to be a place where meaning is never constant, where one reality would blur into another, where maybe, the Wishing Machine sitting in the corner would actually work" (Cardiff). Like most of Cardiff's works, the visitor becomes part of the artwork, for the sounds are only activated as one passes along. As a result the visitor feels a part of the installation, or as if she or he is participating in an ongoing lifestory. Here, in this installation, the viewer is made very strongly aware of the shifts between the experience of common reality and her own projections, fantasies and desires.

In *The Dark Pool* we clearly see how form and expression are means for creating an impression and fulfilling basic needs, although perhaps only a little. In this sense a performance can be "world creating", bestowing insight, or evoking action, or encouraging some kind of personal healing.

In this way a performance may lead to the core of the spiritual, helping us in the search for insight into our existence, helping us to cope with our "suffering and longing" and giving us reason to hope for a future that accords more closely with our ideal of the just and good life.

In the course of my observations I have developed what I call a rule of religious or moral performance. This rule can be demonstrated in terms

Figure 2.4. Janet Cardiff (collaboration with George Bures Miller),
The Dark Pool, 1995, in: C. Christov-Bakargiev, *Janet Cardiff.
A Survey of Works Including Collaborations with George Bures Miller*,
PS1.MoMA, Long Island City 2001, p. 53

of two examples: first, the effect of an evening at a comedy club, and second, Cardiff's *The Dark Pool.*

A *spectator* (S) attending a comedy performance (P) has *a general sense* (FR) of emptiness, a rather grey mood and a *longing* (L) to have this bad mood be replaced by something more satisfying. By the *method* (M) of performing funny acts and telling jokes (A), the performer creates a sense of fun and cheerfulness that has the *effect* (E) of lifting the spectator's mood.

A visitor (S) entering the door to Cardiff's installation *The Dark Pool* (P) has a general feeling of questioning his identity (FR) and a longing, for enlightenment (L). By jumping into another lifestory (M) with the help of the installation (P) of objects and sounds (A) he comes to feel better about himself and his possibilities in life (E).

In an abstract form, the rule of religious or moral performance looks like this.

"To strive for the effect E on participating students S, who prior to the performance have the personal disposition FR and – mostly unconscious – the individual longing L for satisfaction of a basic need, we might use a selfmade performance P with the method or form M, consisting of the activities or expressive elements A1, A2 etcetera".

2.5. Observation-Spirituality: the Role of Installation Art

Rituals, installations and performances are useful not only in schools, but also in diaconal catechesis for adults. With the help of them we can represent the longing, evoked by the Holy Spirit, to make something good of creation. God, through the working of the Holy Spirit, urges human beings to partake of God's longing for the Kingdom, and to seek to satisfy that longing by acting on behalf of righteousness and goodness for all. The Spirit awakens the longing in us, using every human feeling and possibility, both in words and in deeds. The Spirit uses our personal basic needs and functions to make us 'observant' of our own wishes and the needs of other people. In order to be 'observant' of the needs of others, we must observe and understand those needs in ourselves. Therefore we cannot love the other without really loving ourselves. In Chapter 3 I will argue that Foucault referred to as the "souci de soi" (care for oneself) is the basis for a diaconal mentality, since our innermost feelings, desires and longing, of which we are often not fully aware, are generally very similar to those of other people, people who, like ourselves, suffer and feel an unbearable emptiness.

In the following explanation how to work with installations in school and in church I make use of examples of existing works of art. Here we must listen to Job Koelewijn who never yielded to the well-intended invitation to present his *Cleaning the Rietveld Pavilion* elsewhere. Although this work has universal traits, it is dependent on the vernacular environment for its effect. Had he presented this performance anywhere else, he would have violated his own principles about the role of context in a work of art. Therefore, when a work of art is used for a purpose other than the one originally intended by the artist and in another context, *it is no longer art.*

My aim is to use the underlying possibilities of works of art for my own rule of performance without pretending to produce art. Nevertheless, some works present particular ethical problems, in which case they are best left alone.

My project requires a type of school and church where children and adults learn to see, to experience and to live with the paradox mentioned earlier, so excellently portrayed by Roy Rappaport and Susanne Langer[15]: the paradox between empirical reality as observed by our five senses on the one hand, and on the other hand everything imagined and expressed by human beings that makes life worth living for us. Children must learn to develop their own imagination by being offered a broad range of opportunities for metaphorical thinking and bodily feeling. Unfortunately this kind of education is not currently considered a priority in my country, and there is little or not training for teachers and pastors in this approach. They need the help of art teachers. Another consideration I only mention in passing is the need to take into account the level of cognitive and social development of children and what kinds of methods and materials would be most suitable at various stages[16].

To work with students and church members in this way is not inherently difficult. Ideas may be found by browsing in the art section of a bookshop. For my classes I choose, say, 15 photographs of installations that are in some way suitable for the subject of the lesson that is currently under way. These are given to the group. Each member of the group makes his or her own choice and defends this choice with good arguments about the content or subject, the possibilities of the installation, the different competences of the group members and – in a school setting – possible links with other subjects like computer, art, music and handicrafts. Then the group chooses the installation they will use as an example.

All of my examples follow the rule of performance mentioned above. I bear in mind the circumstances and the basic needs of each participant, as far as it is possible in the learning situation. The rule must express the method and the anticipated outcome. It must also predict the most likely effects and the form in which the performance will be realized.

The most effective way to learn about existential matters is by direct involvement in the subject. I remember to Schulze's statement, that we live in an experience society. Therefore, to teach in an existential way, we must look for the personal basic needs and experiences of the group members and use these as a basis for learning.

So the examples below must be in tune with the five intentions regarding spiritual observing I described in this chapter:

a. The examples must be congenial with some of the five outcomes of a spiritual teaching-learning process identified in section 2.1. Then a first condition for success is to start from the lived experiences of the group members.

b. The objectives of this didactical method go beyond the common aims of acquiring cognitive and emotional insight. Depending on the subject, the teaching-learning process must include, in the long-term, each of the six domains of basic experiences relating to basic needs and functions, I have summed up in section 2.4.

c. The works are neither purely cognitive-discursive nor purely symbolic in nature. They contain the paradox of rituals, which also means that the performers of a work never try to encode its inner meaning entirely.

d. In connection with c, the exterior of the work is merely the form, which should be transparent to what is interior to it. Beautiful aesthetics may be helpful for rendering the inner significance of a work, but they can also darken the meaning. The purpose is not to create beauty, but to create ritual.

e. During the work of preparing for, creating and performing the project, the teacher or pastor encourages the members of the group to use every intellectual and other mental capacity and every bodily skill that will contribute to the desired outcome.

Work No. 1: Drawing the Line

The first example comes from a Canadian artists' group. Art critic Christopher Reed describes it this way: "Perhaps the best example of art at the intersection of feminist community, sexual identity, postmodernist deconstruction of meaning and the censorship controversies that together characterize the art world at the turn of the nineties is the work of the collective "Kiss and Tell" from Vancouver. Their installation, *Drawing the Line*, presents 100 photographs of lesbian sexuality, arranged from less to more controversial"[17]. Visitors are given pens and asked to record their comments as a kind of wall discussion (figure 2.5).

This piece can serve as a simple starting point for an installation on any subject that is currently being studied. Taking into consideration the importance of direct experience for existential learning, it may serve, for example, as the starting point for a debate on the rights and wrongs of a colonial war waged by the students' own country, and a discussion of the consequences in the present. In the Netherlands we have not only the depths of our colonial war in Indonesia after World War II, but also the multicultural implications of colonialism today. After the war, war is not yet over; anyhow, Shalom is not the same as no-war.

Figure 2.5. Installation *Drawing the line*, 1990;
Collective "Kiss and Tell", Vancouver; in: N. Stangos (ed.),
Concepts of Modern Art, London 1994, p. 138 (Photo Isabelle Massu 1990)

In chapter 6 I discuss the use of this type of artwork, a wall discussion, for the subject "A drop-in center".

Work No. 2: Jacqueline Fraser, A Portrait of the Lost Boys

Fraser lives in New Zealand. *A portrait of the lost boys, 'in five parts deftly and six details of straining'*, is an installation of fabric, wire and text. It consists of five stands with the same figuration but different subjects, though on the same theme. It has the elegance of high fashion, but its beauty and fragility is deceptive. "Beneath the surface appeal lies a sharp critique of our tendency to form cultural stereotypes despite the increasingly global nature of society"[18]. Her work is often about people who do not 'fit in' because of race, class, economic status, or culture. In this work "the drama unfolds through a series of eleven wire female figures, shrouded in black net veils, pinned above or below the heads of young boys. Despite the work's seductive beauty, the text on the light-box reveals the underlying narrative of the horror of self-inflicted death: 'To Our Lost Boy Ivan, carbon monoxide gassed 1998'." Under each set of figures, texts with poems and names of several countries describe acts of violence and despair. Fraser knows that it can take place in any country.

Groups working on themes like "torture", "women and incest", "refugees", and so on, could use this work as a basis for personal creative reflection. For example, they might illustrate a number of facts gathered by Amnesty International with "parts and details" that they have assembled on a series of stands that look similar but contain different facts.

An 'excluded' example: Judy Chicago's The Dinner Party

Another work that can serve as an inspiration for numerous similar performances is the famous installation *The Dinner Party* by Judy Chicago, 1974-1979. The triangular table both denies a hierarchical seating arrangement and suggests female sexual identity. Chicago designed 39 place settings, each celebrating the life and work of a famous woman. Underneath the table are a further 999 names of supporting women.

My idea, based on Chicago's work, was to place Israelis, Palestinians and Jordanians (or three other nations or groups in conflict) along each of the three sides, with characteristic elements of the respective group decorating the place-mats.

Ultimately, however, I concluded that *The Dinner Party* was too much a monument of feminist art[19], and that out of respect for the significance of the piece it should not be reproduced, however respectfully, in the service of other ideas. In my view certain works of art are beyond this kind of alteration and instrumentalization, and it is ethically unacceptable to make use of them for didactical performances. Zadkine's *The Destruction of Rotterdam* I would also place in this category.

Conclusion

In this chapter I presented my vision of longing for the just and good life. This longing is most readily visible in religion, in art and in nature. Happiness, beauty and a 'just world without end' cannot be grasped in words, though much has been written about them. As Gadamer says, beauty can only be experienced as mystery in an act of creativity, and the same goes for truth and justice[20]. All humankind has the mental ability to long, and so to strive for the just and good life. We can encourage this ability when we teach each other to act creatively and to perceive in new ways. One way of teaching this kind of perceptions is through the use of existing artworks. We 'fill' methods and forms of those works with other intentions, our own subjects. I want to stress again that it is necessary to use subjects that present the lived experiences of the group, for only if people's own open or hidden needs are awakened will they be open to the often unbearable needs of others. In this way the congregation can grow in diakonia, in willingness and readiness for the ministry of mercy and justice.

That is the subject that will be discussed in the next chapter.

CHAPTER 3.

DIAKONIA: CONSCIOUSNESS-RAISING
*Expending Social Concern
and Outreach in the Congregation*

3.1. Introduction: Ways of Observing

Late 1991
Ted Turner made a condensed version of CNN's report on Operation Desert Storm, eliminating almost all trace of protest against the Gulf war, and constructing a narrative frame around George Bush's career and his historic gamble in the Gulf. The frustrations of the Vietnam War were forgotten in this "utopian replay of World War II, fulfilling all the fantasies of victory through overwhelming air superiority" (figure 3.1). Turner used Saddam Hussein's eye, treating it, "by the miracle of video graphics, as the frame for a ninety-second run-through of Arab 'history' and 'grievances'. Time magazine named Turner the Man of the Year, declaring him to be the 'Prince of the Global Village' for his revolutionizing of television news and praising CNN as the 'beacon of freedom' that will force 'despotic governments to do their bloody deeds, if they dare, before a watching world'"[1].

11/9/2001
They did dare, and we could do nothing but watch.

Some weeks later
As I sit in my armchair in front of the fireplace in a warm, cosy room, drinking tea, I watch the world news. The United States if fighting a war against terrorism. The president is on television: in Bush we trust. Military installations in Afghanistan are being bombed. Only installations,

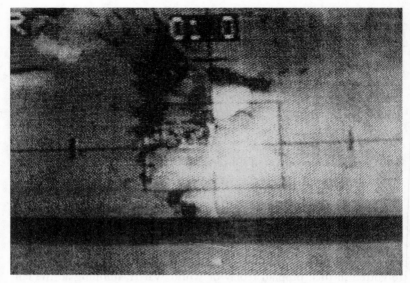

Figure 3.1. *Ground zero* (1991), photo by Nadine McGann from
CNN's Operation Desert Storm, in: W.J.T. Mitchell, *Picture Theory*,
Chicago & London 1994, p. 398

not people, let alone civilians. All I see on the television is clouds of dust
where an explosion has taken place. Then fleeing people, and crying children. The Americans are doing the right thing. The refugees will be able
to go home, the children will stop crying. I have seen what is happening
in the world, the fire is warm and the tea is delicious.

In the preceding chapters we began exploring connections between the
feelings and life experiences of postmodern people in the experience society, and a worldview which is characterized by the longing for righteousness and goodness, expressed in leitourgia and diakonia. This longing, I
believe, is a mental disposition, given to humankind by the Holy Spirit[2].
Everybody can long for the just and good life.

I have suggested that the aestheticization of the lifeworld means that
modern and postmodern people are very concerned with fulfilling their

own postmaterial wishes. If Christians want to celebrate the love of God (leitourgia) and love of their neighbour (diakonia), they will start by envisioning the basic needs and postmaterial wishes of themselves and of each individual person, and then try to transfigure the personal perspective into a wider horizon. For the Holy Spirit longs with us and 'in' us. So we can see our needs and wishes in the light of the just and good life, the vision of the Kingdom of God, a vision, expressed in the parables of Jesus and the charter of diakonia in the church.

Here, I examine the Dutch diaconate, and the way deacons can observe need. Diakonia, and the office of deacon in the sense that it exists in Protestant congregations in the Netherlands, is not well known in other countries. When I talk about the work of deacons, I do so in the sense this word is used in the Dutch Reformed Church. By "diaconal" work I refer to social action by deacons and their cooperators. In this chapter I put myself, so to say, in the deacon's shoes. I hope that not only the deacons, but also other members of the congregation develop their consciousness with regard to the ministry of mercy and justice. I suggest that this is possible by combining 'para-communities' with 'conventional' congregations.

The intended process of consciousness-raising in the church has its origin in aesthetic means in the broadest sense: in 'aisthesis' as observing need. Two examples illustrate this process.

Art critic Lucy Lippard describes a ritual, entitled *The Desert People*, presented by Miriam Sharon at Ashoda Harbor, Tel Aviv in 1978. The performers wore desert costumes in which the head and body were covered in long pieces of cloth similar to the loose skins of animals. Sharon intended "a ritual process to reestablish bonds between people and nature, the relationships of nomadic tents and dwellings to the land, and the political struggle of the Bedouins in the Israeli desert to maintain a way of life that is under attack by modern bureaucracy".[3]

Another perspective on observing need and searching for justice is presented in the work the American art scholar W.J.T. Mitchell, whose comments on Ted Turner were quoted at the start of this chapter. His picture theory is extremely valuable in terms of a teaching-learning process about observing[4], e.g. his remarks on and rediscovery of the original *Duck-Rabbit-picture* (figure 3.2). His observations on CNN's coverage of *Operation Desert Storm* during the Gulf War in 1991 are equally applicable to CNN news coverage of the *Strike Against Terrorism* in 2001 as well as to most Dutch and German television programs on this latest 'strike'.

9. Duck-Rabbit, detail from page in *Fliegende Blätter* (1892).

Figure 3.2. *Kaninchen und Ente*, from Fliegende Blätter (1892), in: Mitchell, p.55f.

Mitchell makes use of a book of CNN's air war consultant, Major General Perry Smith. Smith points out that specific the role of CNN in the media war was "exactly analogous to the Air Force's role in the Gulf. After the first few days CNN achieved total air superiority over the networks". Mitchell: "It provided saturation bombing of the American public with instant analysis (…). It offered 'balanced' debates of the issues between far right hawks" and more moderate hawks, "and rigorously excluded the views of anti-war representatives." General Smith's book is called *How CNN Fought the War*, not how it reported the war; and Smith was their major consultant. "Indeed, this may well be the first time a major American television news network has so openly collaborated with the propaganda machine of the U.S. military", writes Mitchell. He knows that this strategy is common when politicians must try to convince the public. "The main effect was the transformation of a divided, skeptical American public into consensus of passive acceptance and image consumption."

Mitchell's writing is an excellent example of "daring to observe" what is really going on. Though he ends his comments with his own hesitations about the possibility of developing critical public observation. Anyhow, he stresses the need to do it very carefully, and to avoid the "great temptations of melodrama and paranoia". "The task of cultural criticism in this place and time is far from clear". These last sentences the reader and the author of this very study on diakonia have to take to heart themselves.

3.2. Diaconate in the Bible and in Church history. Developments in Thinking about Diaconate, 1950-2002

"I give you a new commandment: love one another; as I have loved you, so you must love one another" (John 13:34).

"If you love only those who love you, what credit is that to you? Even sinners love those who love them. Again, if you do good only to those who do good to you, what credit is that to you? Even sinners do as much

(...). But you must love your enemies and do good; and lend without expecting any return (...). Be compassionate as your Father is compassionate" (From Luke 6:32-36).

These words of Jesus form the basis of diakonia in the congregation. Diakonia is a Christian term for the active, reciprocal relations between people who long for the correction or elimination of unbearable material or socio-psychological need. Such relations are not restricted to the congregation, but also enclose the relations of the church members with 'outsiders', according to Jesus even "your ennemies"; everybody, "however humble" (Matthew 25:40). These texts, along with a few others, form the core of biblical teachings about diaconate[5].

The difference between diaconate, natural help lent by family and friends, and other secular forms of assistance or relief becomes clear when we look closely at these texts. The difference between these three types of help would not be evident to an outsider. Thus the difference does not lie in the inherent superiority of Christian help. The difference consists in four aspects: motivation by the Holy Spirit; the Christian vision of life and society; the Christian view of mankind as created "in the image of God"; and the hope, the longing for the fulfillment of righteousness and goodness in the Kingdom of God[6].

From the selection of texts mentioned above we can put together three *biblical maxims about diaconate*.

First, in the Tenach and Gospel – the Old and New Testament – it is understood that people within the community where the Lord, the God of Israel is worshipped, will look after each other because God has looked after us first. Looking after each other takes place in a spiritual as well as in a material sense. Jesus said that the Kingdom of God happens where people do not reign, but serve. Each of us is dependent on others and responsible for others. This is the principle of mutuality. Second, faithfulness, righteousness and love are the basic notions of diaconate. Third, the Bible tells us that God has mercy on the poor. A child of God knows that by helping even one poor person we help God. The poor are the prototype of human beings in need, who in the Bible also are referred to as strangers, widows or orphans.

These three starting points, though of course endorsed, where already too strict for the practice in the first Christian churches. They mostly restricted their help to members of the congregation, and in doing so they weakened the three elementary notions with respect to diakonia. They often forgot the principle of mutuality; they did not look for the stranger and did not see the poor as the icon of God[7].

Sometimes the biblical texts can be taken literally, but in most cases we must translate their meaning for our (post-) modern context. This is the case, for example, with texts about the position of slaves, strangers and people with handicaps, about sexual behavior and gender, and so on. Today we also have other ideas about human rights and responsibilities, especially about the obligations of the rich and of people with much knowledge. A judgment of biblical texts has not only to do with relevant exegesis for our time (which we call hermeneutics A), but also with the faith, the philosophy of life and existential life experience of all persons involved in diaconate, not least the poor themselves (hermeneutics B), as emphasized in the report by the American Presbyterian Church, *Hope for a Global Future*[8].

Historical developments in diaconate

The highest ideal of the Kingdom of God, 'not ruling but serving' (Matthew 20:25f), that is expressed in the three maxims, seemed unrealistically high even at the time the New Testament was written. The trend continued in the Catholic Church. In the Middle Ages the churches in general did not set themselves aside from the world of government and power, of 'ruling'; on the contrary, churches themselves wielded a great deal of worldly power, economic and often political as well. The ideal, 'serving' church was restricted to holy orders in monasteries and convents. Diaconate became for the most part caritas, welfare for the poor, within ecclesiastical systems of power. But there have always been counter-movements like the Ebionites, the Franciscans, Thomas Münzer, the 'Social Gospel' and the so-called Basic movements from about 1970 onward.

John Calvin emphasized "fides et caritas", the unity of faith and love. He wanted a serving church and gave back to the office of deacon, who had become a theologian and a clergyman in the Catholic Church, its original meaning. In the Calvinist tradition, the office of deacon is tied to the ministry of the poor. The deacon is officially called, chosen and sent by the congregation.[9]

Most Protestant congregations today do not have an office of deacon. In Calvinistic churches the situation varies. In the Presbyterian Church in the United States, for example, it is up to the congregation to choose whether to make use of the office of deacon,[10] though the idea of working for justice is greatly honored[11].

The situation in the Netherlands is different from that in other European countries. In Germany, for example, structural "diaconal" work is carried out by large Protestant and Catholic associations that promote social welfare on behalf of the whole nation. In the Netherlands social welfare is almost entirely secularized and is the responsibility of the public authorities. Congregations and parishes are seldom involved in caring for the poor. The identity of the diaconate of the local church, so firmly articulated by Calvin, is very unclear at this moment. Nevertheless there are still formal structures for the work of the deacons in each congregation; deacons gather money for world projects and for 'small help' to church members undergoing financial problems, often called 'help under protest' because of the failing governmental social security system.

Sometimes congregations will undertake or participate in private initiatives to provide help for refugees, the homeless, drug users or other outsiders who receive little or no social and financial support from local or state government.

This work in the ministry of mercy and justice, though carried out with the gifts of the congregation, is for the most part not strongly supported by the majority of the chuch members. There are usually some 'activists' who are involved in this kind of work, but the rest of the members are often not interested or even rather sceptical about helping strangers and 'outsiders' who may be seen as 'lazy' or otherwise undeserving. The congregation often has little understanding of or sympathy for the three maxims with regard to diakonia. Nevertheless, I believe it is possible to develop this sense. At this particular juncture, people in our Western societies are open to post-material values, and for Christians this also means that there is an opportunity for a change in social consciousness.

In this chapter I describe diaconate and observing need from the perspective of the deacons and their cooperators. I will suggest formal steps to further the growth of social consciousness in the congregation. I discuss the forms of resistance to awareness of diakonia and the possibilities of 'para-communities' in the field of diakonia. In the remainder of the book I will draw on the ideas presented in the first chapters to explore ways of encouraging a more concrete and committed attitude of the whole congregation towards diaconate.

3.3. Learning to Observe Need

The German practical theologian Steinkamp has suggested that observing need cannot be taken as a matter of course. We all have our private biases and presuppositions that interfere with aisthesis. We choose the need we can handle, for we cannot bear the burden of all the world's misery on our shoulders. Moreover, according to Steinkamp, we would do well to listen first to the French philosopher Foucault, who reminds us of the classic notion of "le souci de soi", care for oneself[12]. If people do not care for themselves in a fundamental way or if they carry around troubles, they are themselves a source of troubles, a sign of human lack. Foucault mentions three things people need with regard to "le souci de soi". First, human beings need sufficient material resources to maintain life, and preferably enough to allow them to enjoy life. Second, being social creatures, we need strong relationships with family and friends, and the knowledge and attitudes to survive and thrive in our own culture. Third, we need to learn from childhood that people always have to live with obstacles and lack. Therefore we conclude that human beings have basic material needs like need for food and shelter, immaterial needs like the

need for trust and love, and, according to Inglehart, today we also wish
to deal with a lot of postmaterial values such as social prestige or the lust
of travel.

Only when our own "souci de soi" is satisfied can we open ourselves
up to observing the need of others. But the possibility of openness does
not yet mean that we truly observe need. It is only a necessary condition.
So now I turn to the question: How can we learn to observe need?

The best way to learn to observe need is to have direct experience of
situations of need and suffering. Where such direct experience occurs,
learning occurs quickly and thoroughly. But where direct experience is
absent, it may be necessary to create artificial situations of contact with
people who are in need. Sometimes we can imitate a real context of people in distress and need by so-called interactive theatre in which participants, together with professional actors, take on the roles of people in
marginalized situations. This is very expensive, so in many cases we have
to learn about the problems faced by people in need without their real or
'acted' presence. This can be done by role-playing, or, as suggested here,
by the use of artworks. For both cases I propose the following statement:
Christians believe that their own material and immaterial basic needs are
created not only to stimulate their physical and mental skills, so that they
can fulfill their own "souci de soi", their own – legitimate! – egocentric
longing for the just and good life, but also to allow them to understand
and feel the needs of every other human being.

The learning process with the help of an artwork, making together a
performance, is only possible in a group that forms a kind of community. In a community people are equal; where people encounter each other
on an existential level equality is a matter of course. This is true as well of
situations in which Christians encounter each other. In the church, relationship starts from faith, the grace of God in Christ by the Holy Spirit.
But this remains a hollow phrase until people experience themselves as
equal and are struck by the existential sense of the presence of God. God
is the one who knows human suffering, distress and want, who experienced human misery in the humility of Christ, Christ who "in obedience
accepted even death – death on the cross" (Phil. 2: 8). The experience of

this event, for Christians the most important since creation, put life in an entirely new light for Jesus' disciples. From then on they experienced longing for justice and goodness. The Holy Spirit also fills us with yearning for this new life in which outsiders and strangers in need become our sisters and brothers. The teaching-learning process that I propose starts from this idea: to learn within a group where the members can feel a sense of community because they experience that God yearns for the elimination of human suffering and want.

In a true Christian group the members, who all bring to the encounter their own needs, experience together the suffering of Christ. This communal experience also can heighten their personal consciousness of the suffering of marginalized people, if they live their situation, even if those people are not present. In the next chapters I give examples of this way of learning by using aesthetic performances and installations. Here, I conclude this section with some remarks on community.

The process of learning to become aware of the suffering and want of others, which I call learning to 'observe need', can create very close bonds among the members of the group, much closer than the bonds created among the community of church members in worship. This is because an experience that is 'undergone' in a group situation can be especially intense and have a stronger impact on individuals than things which are experienced when one is alone. A group member experiences his or her own existential material and immaterial needs more intensely when they are talked about, reflected on and felt in a group, as the group becomes conscious of individuals suffering an unbearable lack. This was the outcome of a small project carried out by a group of students that will be discussed in Chapter 6.

A true Christian community is a community, conscious of diakonia, of the ministry of mercy and justice. In the Lord's Supper this community experiences together the suffering of Christ (*anamnesis*, remembrance), and the longing and preparation for his Second Coming with the help of the Spirit (*epiclese*, the call for the Spirit). According to the Bible it is essential for the celebration of the Lord's Supper that a community is involved in diakonia. Therefore an 'ordinary' congregation that lacks this consciousness is not a real koinonia. Though all members of a congregation may privately be in favour of diakonia, most of them will not or cannot be active in a group involved in social action. Groups, involved in social action, and other groups that keep the spirit of a congregation alive, will be referred to as 'para-communities' and will be discussed in more detail in section 3.8.

3.4. Five Steps to Consciousness with regard to Diakonia in the Congregation[13]

Consciousness with regard to diakonia, in the congregation, can be fostered by implementing the following five steps.

The first step is listing and classifying existing activities on mercy and justice in the congregation. Part of this step of raising awareness consists in facing the reality of one's own position, social, economic and otherwise. In Dutch Protestant churches there are three offices, namely the (professional) minister of the Word of God (preacher), (voluntary) elders and deacons. The deacons, usually three or four, form the diaconate and organize the corresponding activities. A typical congregation in a Dutch town might have six fields of action with respect to diakonia, consisting of 1) attention to the needs in the members of congregation (assisting elderly members, the sick, handicapped people, providing incidental material help, organizing coffee-meetings and meals for lonely people), 2) attention to the needs of others in town, 3) a third-world shop, 4) an Amnesty International committee, 5) a committee on illegal refugees and 6) collection of the offertory and the service, conducted by the deacons, at the Lord's Supper.

The second step is to search for connections between these concrete activities and the aim of diaconate, for example how the biblical contexts can be related to our own time, how we can show care and mercy by our actions, or give a voice to those who are never heard.

In a third step we verify that the groups at whom the activities on mercy and justice are directed are themselves partners in these activities.

For example, we give elderly people the chance to speak out about their perceptions of the care shown them. Refugees staying in the guest room of the church express their own wishes. The members helping the deacons, for example those who help in the kitchen or who collect donations, should have a say in those aspects of decision-making that affect their work. Similarly, the deacons are not merely only executors of liturgical formulas, but have a part to play in the making of the liturgical order.

In a forth step the board of the congregation, first and foremost the deacons with their assistants, together with the elders and the minister, draw up an annual plan setting out the congregation's policy and activities in the ministry of mercy and justice.

The fifth step is the execution of the congregation's policy with regard to diakonia. This may mean restructuring the "diaconal" work in areas that are not in keeping with the policy that has been agreed on.

The entire process of promoting awareness of diakonia should preferably take place within a fairly short time span. It must be carried out under the direction of the board, since it affects policy and activities in all aspects of parish life. Decisions about some aspects of the annual plan must also be discussed with the church members outside the board, as the deacons do according to step three and four of their plans.

In section 3.8 I will discuss the relation between pioneers on social action and traditional church members who do not participate in such activities. Their relations should be fair and both groups need to understand one another. Resistance to the ministry of mercy and justice, which has often psychological and socio-political aspects, will be discussed below.

3.5. What Follows After the Process of Awakening: Encounter and Participation

The process of learning to 'observe need' is important and necessary for every church member, and it is too often neglected. It is the theme of this book. However, once need has been observed and identified, the "diaconal" work itself does not occur in isolation. Much of it takes the form of personal contact with the people who need help. These encounters take time, and only members who are motivated by a strong awareness of the meaning of diakonia, should participate. People in pain should not be exposed to church members who are merely seeking to satisfy their curiosity about certain marginalized groups.

Encounters with those in need may consist of spontaneous meetings, for example talking to 'strangers' participating in meals or the like, of direct, organized encounters with people in need, for example refugees, or of encounters through media such as film, video, internet and the teaching/learning processes with the help of performances I discuss in this study.

If we really meet people who are suffering, we will be moved to participate in social action. To make the most of that motivation once it has been awakened, it is important to pay attention to the relation between those participating actively in the ministry of mercy and justice and the other members of the congregation. In section 3.8 we will see how good relations between the two groups can further the public consciousness of the church members.

The bond between church and society can also be strengthened by "political observing and pointing out". Deacons and their cooperators who are active in this area, and 'help under protest', attend demonstrations, rallies or other events of groups, usually secular, that fight for political and economic rights for marginalized and disadvantaged members of society.

This part of the work of the deacons fulfils a function similar to that of social workers who may be 'present' only in a certain area, to provide support to their clients or to 'give them a voice' (section 4.4).

3.6. Towards a Congregation which Feels Involved in the Ministry of Mercy and Justice

Through consciousness-raising, encounter, participation and 'political observing and pointing out', we can work in a directed way toward encouraging forms of commitment to the church in which desinterested involvement and solidarity with the marginalized and disadvantaged can take shape. In this manner a path becomes visible along which a congregation can develop itself from an inwardly-oriented group to a community aimed at the original goal of looking forward and striving for the Kingdom of God, i.e. a community marked by leitourgia and diakonia, and so a real koinoia.

We can only proceed in this direction if we want to be "a community, born of need", as our late friend and worker in the field of diakonia, Annie Kolk called it[14]. I mentioned before that this kind of community remains something we strive for, and that aspects of realization, shaped like para-communities, are mostly temporarily. Typically, such a para-community is not directed towards its own survival. On the contrary, it should properly aim at making itself unnecessary. After all, the goal of this community is the decreasing or even diminishing of suffering and need, so that the people who are helped can once again stand on their own feet. A community in the ministry of mercy and justice never is an aim in itself, but a temporary means to an end.

People join such a para-community voluntarily. Nothing and no one can oblige them to stay when they want to stop making their contribution. But for people suffering from want and need, it can be disastrous when the community that helps them collapses too early. For this reason it is important that the policies and procedures, the planning, the communication strategies and so on in a group, involved in diakonia, be handled very carefully. And the voices of the people that the group sets out to help must weigh heavily.

The role of the deacon and other laypeople involved in social work

The role of the worker in the ministry of mercy and justice can be characterized in many ways. He or she is the porter, who takes cares that the door of the church stands wide open to respond to the needs of human being and of society. People in need who stand outside the congregation can freely enter, to form the center of pastoral-social care within the congregation. The result is that the heart of the congregation is renewed, in the sense that the poor and needy form literarily and figuratively the center.

The deacon can also be what is in Greek the paracletos (and John calls the Holy Ghost our paracletos), and in Latin and English the advocate, of the marginalized, the people without power and means to assert their rights. Amnesty International, for example, currently acts as an advocate for the Darish women of India.

Another role of the deacons and their cooperators is 'simply' to be present among people who are suffering and in need. This role is sometimes combined with socio-cultural education. In both cases the deacon forms a bridge between the marginalized and disadvantaged outside and the members of the congregation. The deacons take the side of the suffering and needy, and they challenge the other members of the congregation to make their own choices.

As a rule, deacons and their cooperators are highly motivated to help people in need and are prepared to devote a great deal of time to this work. There are two dangers inherent in this. The first is what is sometimes called "helper syndrome", which includes a complex of motives that can be harmful to both the helper and the helped. Some of these are that the helper exercises power over the helped; the helper may encourage dependency among those he helps; the helper may have a desire, generally unconscious, to be seen as good; and the helper may even seek social success through this work, at the expense of those he helps. The aforementioned "souci de soi" is a good insurance against such harmful motivations, as a person who cares for herself does not need to help others for her own sake. Ideally, the helper and the helped will be partners; though the helper may gain many benefits from the activity of helping, this is never an aim in itself. A 'good' helper knows that he himself will one day need help, and those who are helped should know that some day they will be able to another person. This is the principle of mutuality.

The second problem concerns the position of the deacons and their cooperators within the congregation. Often those who are involved in diakonia avoid communicating with the congregation as a whole because of the lack of commitment of most of the members. This is an area, however, in which change is absolutely essential. The gap between those who are active in diaconate and those who are not is a wide one, and it must be bridged instead of widened further. There are many forms of resistance to the ministry of mercy and justice, as outlined in the following, and we must have the courage to observe what is going on around us and to deal with these resistances.

3.7. Resistances and Impediments with regard to Diakonia

Without people who are suffering and in need, there would be no need for diaconate. Ironically, to learn to be a congregation involved in diakonia, we need the poor and the marginalized, and we need to observe them.

A para-community of mercy and justice can form around an individual refugee or refugee family. A community of mercy and justice can only take shape if the community knows that the people who need help 'exist' either inside or outside the congregation. Sometimes we know that people need help but we prefer to help them 'in silence' so as not to shame them. The fear that those who are helped will feel ashamed is understandable, because smugness and condescension are humiliating to people who need help. But by helping silently we affirm the notion that poverty and dependence are cause for shame. If, on the contrary, we believe that poverty is a form of injustice, then work in the ministry of mercy and justice is undertaken in a spirit of solidarity with the victims. The people who are suffering are placed in the center of the congregation. The church will be the place to which they can bring their marginal situation, their material and often also mental need for God. Jesus warned his disciples not to despise the poor, the sick, the sorrowful, but to see them as blessed by God. The church, the Body of Christ, must have the same attitude toward the poor.

Therefore we must 'dare to observe' the invisible and therefore unreachable marginalized. Not daring to observe is an impediment to being a congregation involved in diakonia. Not daring to observe often has to do with the fact that we did not take care of ourselves before. Many

Christians think that 'denying oneself' means to negate the "souci de soi", when in fact taking care of oneself is a condition for being able to be open to other people.

Resistance

Spee[15] discerns three kinds of resistance to a positive attitude regarding the ministry of mercy and justice; social, psycho-social and ecclesiastical.

Social resistances are based on our social and political ideas about the reasons for ills such as poverty, hunger and addiction. If we enjoy a reasonably comfortable social and economic position, we often think, consciously or unconsciously, that we have deserved this position by virtue of our own efforts, be it as an individual or as a nation, and by following the norms and values of our society. We suspect most people who are in position of unbearable suffering of not adhering to the "respectable" ways of doing things. While this may be true in some cases, the suffering is not diminished as a result. The majority of people in positions of need and suffering are not there by any fault of their own. By birth or by circumstances beyond their control, they live under conditions of economic and cultural disadvantage. In the Netherlands, for example, the difference between those with highest incomes and those earning the lowest wages or receiving social security payments has grown considerably in the last twenty years. This widening gap means more (relative) poverty and more poor people.

Psycho-social resistances are inner attempts to ignore or reject feelings with regard to diakonia. According to Freud's principle of sublimation[16] the attempt to satisfy unconscious desires shapes our social behaviour. Unsatisfied desires help foster nationalism and hatred of others. Intercultural teaching/learning processes are essential for encouraging awareness of these internal psychological attitudes and stimulating a more tolerant and more just society. When people become more aware of the "unanticipated consequences" of their attitudes and behaviours, that is the results that they did not consciously aim to produce, there is a real possibility that they can change those attitudes and behaviours.

Another psycho-social resistance is the deeply rooted anxiety about being confronted with the need of others, with which we are all familiar. This anxiety can apply to pastoral care as well as to social contexts. Other resistances that can occur in the ministry of mercy and justice and that can act as obstacles to authentic encounters are resistance to dealing with people of social classes different from one's own, aversion to people who look unattractive or aggressive, or shame at one's own good fortune in the face of marginalized or suffering people.

Ecclesiastic resistance and impediments

Deacons and their cooperators often lament that it is difficult to motivate many church members to assist in activities with respect to diakonia. The members often know little about the situation of the people who need social support. Some do not want to have to think about or talk about what the suffering of others means for their own faith. Here the gap between going to church and living one's faith is clear. Being a church-goer, a member of a congregation and feeling the comfort of knowing oneself to be under the wings of a loving and merciful God is one thing; living the other half of the Christian faith that requires us to love others – strangers, outsiders, the sick, the old and decrepit, even our enemies, like ourselves is quite another.

Members often hear confusing information about marginalized people. Anyone should be able to live on the minimum wage by managing their money properly. People on welfare spend their money on the wrong things. They are unreliable and dishonest. Why should we help criminals? They must help themselves first. According to this view, people who are in trouble must change first, and then the church can reach out to help them, instead of demanding that the church help them in their confict with an enonomic and social system that has made them what they are.

Another argument against help is that poverty and injustice are political issues, and that it is up to the political authorities to deal with them.
In this view the church is merely adding to the problem by attempting to
alleviate suffering and thereby taking pressure off the political system[17].

A contemporary example in the Netherlands is the new refugee law.
Refugees are accommodated for up to three years in asylum centers located all over the country. If a request for asylum is rejected – often after
years of investigation – the refugee is given a month to arrange the for-
malities for return to the country of origin. At the end of the month he
or she will be taken from the center and deported, with no further rights
or avenues for appeal. Since the law was passed, the number of illegal
aliens in the country has grown by four thousand in half a year. One of
these is a Kurdish woman whose husband abandoned her and their three
children. She cannot return to Turkey because her children have no
Turkish passport. While waiting for her case to be decided, she slept
under a bridge in the cold, wet November weather. A church in Assen
gave her shelter and the municipal council gives her enough money to
live on. And yet many people who support the new law say that we must
not help such people, because then they will think that the Netherlands
are a country where it is easy to live on charity, even as an illegal alien.

Fortunately, as soon as these hardliners actually encounter human
beings in trouble, like the Kurdish woman living under a bridge with her
children, they often change their mind[18]. However, most of these people
will resist encountering this kind of suffering and misery face to face.

All of the forms of resistance described here are also potential sources
of conflict within the congregation. Therefore it is critical to keep the
congregation informed of the church's ministry of mercy and justice, to
ensure open and honest communication between groups involved in
social work and the rest of the congregation, and to resolve conflicts, and
potential conflicts, quickly, calling on outside help if necessary.

Some obstacles such as mutual distrust among elements within the
congregation, or recrimination between church members and the people
with an unbearable lack, require, for example, organizing meetings
among various groups within the congregation, as it may be beyond the

strength or ability of people to defend themselves when they find themselves in difficult situations.

3.8. Para-Communities

In our Handbook, the suggestion is made that congregations needs many kinds of "para-communities". Para-communities are groups, generally small in size, within the congregation, that relate with other members of the congregation as well as with the society at large. In these para-communities the idea of fulfilling spiritual longing through religious or aesthetic experiences can be most clearly expressed.

My collegue Gerrit Immink, from our institute, HTWI, has suggested that we call our ecclesiological model 'the congregation as the riverbed of the spiritual offer of Gods Spirit'. God offers the Spirit, to live with and – even if this goes beyond the metaphor – to move on the congregation. This, in my view, is precisely what a congregation is meant to be. Alas, many existing religious institutions, like the big churches, are rigid and focused primarily on their own internal affairs. They are concerned mainly with surviving or neutralizing the risks of conflicts arising from the rapid change of ideas and values in our culture. They promote a 'feel-good' mentality among their members. This rigidity and clinging to the status quo has led to the formation of many kinds of new Christian groups, from evangelical or charismatic groups, to groups with open and postmodern aesthetic concepts or action groups in the sphere of diakonia.

These widely differing groups have two things in common. They all attempt, in their own particular way, to do justice to the Gospel and to the (post-) modern culture of today's society. Consequently they are often out of place within unworldly or rigid congregations. They are seen as outsiders, and a challenge to the established organization. Instead of rejecting these groups and forcing them to break away entirely from the established churches, we suggest that traditional congregations establish a working bond with individuals or groups with new or unconventional ideas, and encourage them to be active within the congregation as 'para-communities'. The formation of para-communities is a core item of our ecclesiology.

Most members like a traditional congregation where they can find respite from the restless existence in postmodern society. They want to feel safe in Christ, and feel that they are entitled to this safety based on Jesus' words: "Come to me, all whose work is hard, whose load is heavy, and I will give you relief" (Mt 12:28). Yet this is only half of Jesus' message. The other half is that a great many people work hard and carry a heavy load but never find any rest, for reasons ranging from physical or mental illness, addiction and poverty to natural disasters or war. Anyone who has truly found rest in God, the fulfilment of the "souci de soi", cannot help but be aware of a holy unrest about suffering and need in the world.

Many church members, however, experience neither holy rest nor unrest; they believe in a traditional, more extrinsic or social way. Almost always it will be only a small group that feels the holy unrest that God's Spirit will awaken in us. All the more reason, then, for that small group to be cherished by the members of the traditional congregation, who are well aware that they often come over as the church at Laodicea, neither hot nor cold but lukewarm (Rev. 3:15f). John does not write that Jesus rejects people searching for rest, but Jesus wants to show them the just and good life of the Kingdom. Perhaps, there can be more than rest.

With our ecclesiology of the local church we have basically two things in mind. We want to repeat Jesus' word about finding rest in God. Every member must know that she is accepted by God the way she is. Everyone carrying a heavy load will find rest in the congregation. The confidence that God is with us is reason to celebrate, to enjoy the gifts of God's creation. This part of our ecclesiology could be entitled "Enjoying God".

At the same time we hope to pervade every member with the conviction that God wants the good life, justice and peace for every creature. God wants to establish his Kingdom in the midst of humankind, in the midst of us. The church members must realize that the congregation bears a great responsibility for the establishment of the coming Kingdom of God. They need to sustain all those in the community who are moved by the Spirit of holy unrest, so that these people can give form to their desire to establish goodness and justice on earth. The para-communities in the ministry of mercy and justice, formed by these members are, so to speak, the shock troups of the congregation.

Thus our ecclesiology asks for attention to the need of every one of its members for rest, and for the congregation as a whole to be attentive to and sustain members moved by a holy unrest.

The experiences of those who are taking part in the ministry of mercy and justice, for example accompanying a refugee to the immigration police, or going to the welfare office with a welfare recipient, be dealt with in the congregation. Of course, this would be done openly only when the matter was a public one; in all other cases it would be discussed anonymously, i.e. without naming the participants. One of the most effective ways of doing this is as part of the main weekly service, perhaps as part of the announcements and prayers, or in a worship devoted to a special theme, and, of course, by teaching/learning processes to observe the needs of others. Other possibilities are through publications or at meetings of the congregation. Sharing the experiences of the deacons and their cooperators with the whole congregation creates new bonds between the groups, involved in diakonia, and the rest of the members, helping to diminish the estrangement of those groups from the rest of the congregation and clarifying the relationship between the church and public life[19].

The experience of a community in the ministry of mercy and justice, feeling spiritually sustained by a congregation has a great influence on the faith and experience of faith of the group. Biblical narratives, psalms and songs take on a new content and power of expression in the weekly tides of contemplation when a congregation is involved in an activity such as offering refuge in the church to asylum-seekers. This is what Moltmann calls "der Weg vom Text zur Tat", the path from text to action[20].

Why do we call the congregation the riverbed of the spiritual offer of Gods Spirit?

We live in an experience society. So we want to stress the priority of the faith of the faithful, as experienced in (post-) modern society, over hierarchical orders of the church and over the influence of theologians and the clergy. We also want to be realistic, "sober and vigilant" (1 Peter 4:8), about the position of the church in society, and hopeful that the faithful will open themselves up more and more to the spiritual offer of God.

By starting with the Holy Spirit as the origin of diaconate, we make it clear that our model is biased toward a congregation in which professionals – for instance the minister or priest – and volunteers form one team whose members mutually support one another, including in a spiritual respect.

The connection between dogmatics and ecclesiology is very much in evidence here. A *christological* starting point will stress the accomplished work of Christ and in that case the congregation will be inclined to follow their minister or priest as their spiritual leader. Not the 'ordinary' churchmembers, but the minister, takes on something of the role of Christ. A *pneumatological* starting point implies that the whole congregation is awakened, owing to salvation in Christ, to long for the Kingdom and to strive in sacral and profane action for goodness and mercy on earth. Here the minister is not the leader of the congregation, but one of its spiritual counsellors.

Conclusion

One or more socially involved para-communities, born of need, can maintain good relationships with the congregation as a whole, and move it toward becoming a socially involved congregation. Characteristic of such a congregation is that the personal experiences of the poor and suffering play a role in the formulation of the policy regarding the ministry of mercy and justice. A socially involved para-community is a group which acts toward a social purpose, mostly for people outside the congregation, but that maintains strong contacts with the inner sphere of the congregation. Such a para-community will also have its own times of prayer, meditation or worship, and feel very closely bound together. Nevertheless it will generally be of a temporary nature and the group also form relationships with the 'ordinary' congregation. This ecclesiastic model we name a congregation with para-communities.

Sunday worship provides an opportunity for everybody to learn about the work of all elements of the congregation and establish direct contacts. Such a congregation, in which "leitourgia" (liturgy, worship) and "diakonia" (the ministry of mercy and justice) are equally central, we call a real "koinonia tou christou", a community of Christ.

CHAPTER 4.

PROJECTS IN DIAKONIA

Introduction

In this chapter I will present examples of ideas and situations that invite
us to observe or be exposed to circumstances that could and in some cases
did lead to projects in diakonia.

Many postmodern works of art invite or even force the viewer to
become part of the work. In some ways, this is the case for all observing:
by observing, daring to observe, one becomes part of the 'game', as
Cauquelin says. But some postmodern works of art exist only by the
viewer allowing himself to be exposed to them. This is often the case with
the works of Janet Cardiff, as we have seen before. At the end of this book
I will give another example of Cardiff's work that sweeps the viewer's feelings along. Here, I introduce Diana Thater's ideas about transcendence of
everyday life and the involvement of the viewer. At the Dia Center in
New York, Thater showed an enormous installation, *Knots + Surfaces*[1],
that works with light, video and movement. However, the work is
installed on the spot: the space plays an important role in the radiance of
the installation. This work is on "the bee-dance", the way a worker bee
communicates with her fellow workers to let them know that she has
found a new source of food, negotiating space and time in a way that is
outside human experience and therefore fascinating to us. But, though
captivating to Thater and a lot of visitors, "The image is not ultimately
the most important thing – the creation of space is." According to Thater,
"The visitor is part of the installation; transcendence happens everyday
in every kind of space, and my point is that it can happen here and now
with old, ugly technology and the machines buzzing, because that technology forms the image and holds the image and is endemic to it."

In this work, as in many contemporary artworks, the observer is part of the work and can only understand a work by being exposed to it. Similarly, to understand diakonia and how it functions, people need to be exposed to the circumstances that show the need for diakonal projects and suggest how such projects would be helpful. In the following I present various suggestions for how this kind of exposure can be created.

4.1. *The Hidden Town* – A Sociological Citywalk as a Form of "Diaconal" Observing

A group of Dutch sociologists from Erasmus University in Rotterdam, led by Engbersen and Burgers, invites us to see the hidden town of Rotterdam. In their book *De verborgen stad* (The Hidden Town) they present a "sociological citywalk" in which we will see not the well-known tourist sites and historical monuments, but the social contrasts of a modern urban area. As the authors note, "cities are places of great contrasts, often within short distances. A few hundred meters from the prestigious Millennium Tower is St. Paul's Church of Reverend Visser, who befriends homeless people. In Rotterdam the number of homeless is estimated at two or three thousand. The numbers have been on the rise in recent years, due to the policy of cutting back on admissions to closed psychiatric institutions. Many homeless people wrestle with addictions of many kinds. Their very physical presence in the street is enough to give many people a sense of insecurity. Finding a place in the city where they can be taken care of is a problem"[2]. Nearly opposite St Paul's the West Kruiskade begins. "The best day to get to know the Kruiskade is Saturday, the best season is summer. Then we can admire the phenomenon of 'cruising': cars driving slowly, loud music throbbing from the speakers. Everywhere cars are double parked, there is nothing to do but wait patiently. (…) Biking is the best way to get around. The sidewalks are crowded. Saunter and look around."

Like other cosmopolitan cities, Rotterdam has grown enormously as a result of immigration. Today, new immigrants from poor countries like Suriname, Turkey, Morocco, the Cape Verde Islands and the Dutch

Antilles form one third of the population of Rotterdam. Many of them live grouped together with other people from the same country, but some live in mixed areas. "This walk", the authors of the "citywalk" tell us, "aims at showing the social developments in the city of Rotterdam, shaped by the labour market, the composition of the population, facilities, life styles and urban renewal. The stations along the walk illustrate these general developments, sometimes in detail, sometimes on a larger and more impressive scale. It is a walk that lays open the hidden forces that are forming and changing Rotterdam."

I took the Rotterdam citywalk on a quiet day in late summer. The contrasts between the different districts were just as Burgers had described. As I walked through the streets, which were less lively at this time of year, passing small groups of residents, I had the feeling of being an inquisitive outsider, as indeed I was. Yet my presence did not seem to bother people and, unlike in Palestinian Jerusalem, in Harlem, New York or in Berlin-Kreuzberg, I was not chased away by angry onlookers. In the Netherlands, anyone who is not overtly causing trouble can walk freely everywhere by daylight, though robbery and sexual crimes are always a possibility, especially for women.

The contrasts remain: chic Weema Square with its Millennium Tower elbow to elbow with the ragged and derelict homeless, a Surinamian district followed by a Turkish one. Thanks to the description in the "citywalk" one's attention is drawn to details that would otherwise remain unnoticed. "Ethnic" shops and eating places are easy to spot. At the same time, though, the Dutch menu has also become more exotic in many ways, whether people are dining out or at home. In their eating habits the Dutch have become 'globalized' and 'multicultural'. For people living in their own society in a country where they form the autochthonous population, multicultural and ethnic influences are a colourful addition to a familiar lifeworld. Immigrants, however, are strangers in a strange culture. For many, contact with their home culture is essential. A striking feature in the immigrant districts are the satellite TV dishes aimed toward Morocco or Turkey (figure 4.1). The next district on the walk is home to many people living on welfare. The absence of name-plates on the doors

Figure 4.1. Satellite TV dishes in a Rotterdam street aimed toward Morocco.

illustrates their wish to remain anonymous, beyond the reach of welfare investigators or social workers.

The districts on the walk vary from prosperous to poor. The last one on the route is an area of old, run-down housing awaiting renovation and gentrification. This is where the greater part of Rotterdam's ten thousand illegal immigrants live. "The large number of "belwinkels", phone-shops, is characteristic of the district of Delfshaven, whose inhabitants come from all over the world. The plethora of phone-shops is attributable to keen entrepreneurs who cash in on the need of residents to telephone abroad at the lowest rates. A quick glance at the mostly handwritten price lists shows the diversity of countries the proprietors cater to. The presence of these businesses is also evidence that people are not only locally rooted, but wish to maintain close ties with family and friends in all parts of the world."

This part of Delfshaven is right next to the historical Delfshaven district, one of most sought-after residential districts of Rotterdam. The difference between these two worlds is astonishing. To bridge this difference, the local government invited artists to create the *Tovertunnel*, a magic tunnel running between the two districts (figure 4.2-4). Not only does the tunnel link the two parts of Delfshaven, but it has also become a "symbol of the multiplicity and heterogeneity of the modern town of Rotterdam".

I have taken walks like this one in other cities, and found the same curious mixture of cultures and social contexts. Though New York has changed considerably in recent years, the impression is still the same: "The new immigration has altered the landscape in the city. (…) With continuing immigration, new ethnic neighborhoods and ethnic conglomerations have cropped up in every borough. Certain sections of the city have taken on a new cultural character. In Crown Heights and East Flatbush in Brooklyn, for example, West Indian beauty parlors, restaurants, record stores, groceries, and bakeries dot the landscape, and Haitian, Creole and West Indian accents fill the air." Often new neighbourhoods are "amalgans of newcomers from all parts of the world"[3]. "Questions how these newcomers fit in economically and culturally –

Figure 4.2. The Tovertunnel, a magic tunnel between two districts of Delfshaven.

Figure 4.3. The Tovertunnel, Delfshaven, with a view of the not yet renovated new town.

Figure 4.4. The Tovertunnel, Delfshaven, with a view of the renovated old town.

and obtain work and secure shelter – remain as some of the most pressing issues that American society faces (…) though the exit of native whites is leaving gaps for other groups to fill". Life is hard for newcomers, who hope for economic advancement. "Here life is not worth / a rotten guava. / If a hoodlum doesn't kill you / the factory will"[4]

Such a walk could be designed by groups involved in diakonia in almost every town or city, using information provided by the local council and by people knowledgeable about their town or neighbourhood.

The aim is to observe the living conditions, aspirations and cultural differences between inhabitants of different streets or neighbourhoods, to gain new insight in human relations and conditions, to learn to see reality in many ways and from various perspectives. This is a good starting point for making a social map based on unemployment statistics, insight into the working of the welfare office, data on numbers of addicts and types of addiction, programs offering help for people with psychiatric problems or criminal records, streetscapes and parks, nearness to industrial areas, railways or major roads. A next step will be the study of groups of disadvantaged inhabitants.

4.2. "*I have nobody*". The Silent Help. Solitude, Handicap and the Work of Deacons

I have nobody. This sigh is the title of a book by Firet and Hendriks[5] about pastoral care for people who want to remain anonymous. There are many people who feel alone. The needs of people with addictions, of people in transition, of refugees, are well known today, thanks to media focus in these politically charged issues. Many different action groups are busy in these areas. But there are also other groups suffering unbearable need. Often they think "I have nobody". Neither they nor their helpers are the object of public attention.

A congregation that is active in the ministry of mercy and justice will not forget these 'silent' ones. They are people with mental or physical disabilities. They are the huge numbers of lonely people, living on their own or in nursing homes, most of them elderly. A great many volunteers are needed to back up social workers and nursing staff, to stave off loneliness, isolation and helplessness.

The members of the congregation can help, be it in groups, like paracommunities, organized by deacons, or individually. While this kind of help seems straightforward enough – lonely people are not a political issue, everybody agrees that we should help them – a great deal of misunderstanding exists in this area as well.

First, as said before, in the Netherlands, like elsewhere in Europe, there is a tendency to decrease social help by the government, and to mobilize voluntary help from the population. Moreover, there are new insights from social scientists about help to people with mental retardation and physical illnesses. The "model of care" is replaced by the "model of integration in the socalled 'normal' society", to foster autonomy and the "quality of existence" of these people[6]. Anyway here, when people need social, economic and often physical assistance, politics are at stake. In the end of this section I will discuss the implications of this change in politics and social science for the congregation.

A second misunderstanding, not political or scientific, but social and theological, is the way human beings see each other. In particularly in this area of personal assistance, the helper syndrome can manifest in many forms. We need to ask: do we know who these people we are setting out to help really are? Are we prepared to encounter them as individuals? Can we acknowledge the achievements of people who do not meet our society's criteria for success? In his book *Boden unter den Füssen hat keiner* (Nobody is on firm ground)[7], Ulrich Bach describes a paralysed young man whom he meets in a nursing home, who can move only his eyes. On a sheet of glass above the young man's bed lies a book, text side down, so that the young man can read it as he lies in bed. However, he can only read two pages at a time, and then he must wait for someone to turn the pages. Sometimes, if there is no one nearby, he waits for as long as three hours before he can read the next two pages. The young man, his eyes shining, tells Bach, "I read *Das ostpreussische Tagebuch*, it's excellent!" Says Bach, "Seldom in my life have I admired anyone so much as I did this man. What energy one must have to continue to the end of the book, when one has to wait a hundred and fifty times until somebody turns the page. He persevered, through all those times someone entered the room but failed to take notice of him, or when a word or sentence was broken off at the end of a page and he had to wait for hours before somebody turned it" (Bach 1986, 63).

To recognize this as an achievement, we need to accept a definition of success that differs from what our achievement-oriented society demands. This calls for another vision of being human and of human relations, like our vision of diakonia. Emancipation in the normal sense cannot be our goal; we must go beyond emancipation. Not every person can learn to cope, to become independent in the normal sense of the word. Can any of us ever be completely independent? The Gospel speaks about a balance between responsibility and dependency; and every person has to search to find this balance.

The model of integration of people with mental retardation and physical illnesses in society, and the ministry of mercy and justice of the congregation

During the last decennia government and state subsidized institutions where people with mental retardation and others, where people with physical illnesses, lived together, changed their policy from medical and developmental intramural care to the model of integration in society.

People with a physical illness often can live and work rather satisfactory in society owing to the improved medicine. Therefore their problems are mostly unknown to ousiders, accept when their illness increases or when they do not use their medicines, and sometimes become angry. When they are living on their own, they are not 'seen' by any congregation, when they are not a member themselves. This problem is not yet much considered in the church.

Quite another group are people with a mental retardation. They often live on their own now, partly in surrogate family homes, partly on their own, though more or less supervised, all over the country. Here, owing to the social competences of this group, almost every step to integration in society must be guided. But not only good neighbours, family members and friends are needed. The socalled 'normal' population must admit them in their clubs and associations, accept their way of shopping and the like in everyday life, and, moreover, question their own normality.

Diakonia in this field has to do with two things. There need to be members of the church who like to deal part of their free time with people with a mental retardation. The congregation as a whole must be learned to receive them in the way every civilian has to do, in worship and working groups, in short as normal sisters and brothers in Christ.

4.3. Open Houses for the Lonely or Homeless

Trenton, New Jersey: Food for Survival

Ugliness and oppression are connected, like beauty and redemption. These words of South African theologian J.W. De Cruchy[8] rise to the surface of my mind as we enter Trenton, New Jersey. We pass streets of ugly, run-down houses, with unemployed, bored-looking black people. Cultural and economic backwaters exist everywhere in the world and so they do in Trenton. "We don't have many poor people in Princeton, so my wife will take you to Trenton", my collegue Rick Osmer suggested, and I accepted gladly. Without people who suffer there would be no need for diakonia and, oddly, even writing about diakonia needs the poor. So Sally Osmer took me with her to Trenton, where she is the director of an ecumenical organization for the prevention of hunger and homelessness. When I ask her whether she would walk around in this neighbourhood at night, she says she does not even like me to walk around here during the day. Churches have bought six houses in this district, and one of them is Sally's center, subsidized by a number of different churches, especially the Presbyterian Nassau Church – which does have deacons – and the Episcopal Trinity Church of Princeton. She introduces me to a number of the volunteers at the center. Then we go to the food bank. The center also distributes clothing, provides help with budgeting, and offers counselling and other kinds of problem solving, such as paying bills when tenants are about to be evicted.

Before the clients enter we stand in a circle, holding hands, and Annabel, one of the workers in the food bank, prays with us. So the work of diakonia begins in a liturgical setting. I am given a blue apron like the others, with "Crisis Ministry" printed on it. A large group of people is already waiting outside. The food bank opened the previous day and will stay open for two weeks; clients may use the bank once a month. Two workers check clients at the entrance. They give a white card to a single person and coloured cards to people shopping for a family. The colour of the card determines how many 'points' worth of food each person may 'buy'. Signs on the shelves show the name of the product and its point value. A single person gets a frozen TV dinner, a family can take home frozen deer meat. "I don't eat deer, poor animal", someone shouts. It takes me some time to understand the English names of the products and the point system, and I am not the only one. Many of the clients need help. Some cannot read, others, like me, do not understand the points. Some even leave the whole job to the volunteers and one woman says, "I don't mind at all." I am not much use, and I am glad that I find some small jobs like removing plastics, flattening and bundling used cardboard boxes, and giving out frozen meals. Annabel and Susan help the clients who need assistance.

One woman can scarcely stand, but later on I see her in the soup kitchen. She looks very unkempt, like the man who goes to the restroom to wash. These two are dirty and they stink, but they are exceptions. Most of the clients are simply poor. Some look so well-groomed and "middle class" that one wonders what turn of events led them to need a food bank. Sally mentions some reasons: a grandmother of thirty-two, driven out of her home at a young age; women who fled physical and sexual violence with their children. Annabel is one of them. She came as a client, became a volunteer and now has a paid job in the food bank.

I am just beginning to understand the point system when Sally invites me to go with her to the soup kitchen, located in another of the church houses. On the way she gives an old woman from the center a lift to the old-age home. In the car the woman relates part of her story of misery. The soup kitchen is busy, there must be about two hundred people in the dining room. The kitchen serves two meals a day. There are two policemen. One of them explains that their services are requested and paid for by the organizing institution. Usually their mere presence is enough to secure order, but sometimes they need to intervene. He laughs when I tell him they are doing a good job. Privately, though, the presence of police in a place like this strikes me as bizarre. It would never happen in the Netherlands.

The goal of my visit is the room where some visitors take courses in painting. Many of them see themselves as artists, for they sell their paintings, and some of the work is very good. Alice, the art instructor, teaches drawing and painting while at the same time taking care of her 'students'. They display their works on the walls of the dining room. Two large black women with deep voices call to me, pointing out their work on the walls. They are proud of the paintings and collages, which they can and will sell. Indeed, the *Outsider Art Fair*, the premier international art fair devoted to art brut and visionary art, is opening the following week in New York[9], and I think that some of the works produced at this soup kitchen could easily be shown there.

In the small, stuffy room where the art lessons are under way, Alice assigns me a chair, but as soon as she goes out, two women ask me to stand up for they want to work at the table. When I do, though, they simply sit down; this is clearly their spot. A young woman is drawing a picture, and I ask her if it is a farm. She says no, and continues cheerfully, "My granny had a farm in Mercerville, of course you don't know where that is, and she had a lot of chickens and cows." She does not tell me what the drawing represents. A boy carries a big canvas into the room and in no time he completes his painting, consisting of blue background with purple spots, green and yellow stripes and, as a finishing touch, white spirals. His work is ready in half an hour, and he will leave it to dry for the rest of the day. He shows me a smaller painting of his hanging in the dining room, which I like better than the new one. "He has an image of everything he wants to do before he starts", says Alice. We have our picture taken together (figure 4.5a and b). People are constantly going in and out. They do not work for long stretches of time, most of them turn to Alice frequently for attention and seem rather fidgety.

A man who has just come in shows me some of his works: texts written in beautiful handwriting accompanied by naive coloured drawings, most measuring about 20 to 30 cm and sometimes printed on texture. Alice says she especially likes the one with a man behind the netting in the Mercer County Correctional Center in Trenton, talking to a woman on the other side of the netting. It is entitled "Thank you… for being there for me". "This is real", says Alice, "this is from experience", and he agrees. I make a photo of the picture (figure 4.6), which looks like a

Figure 4.5a Painting in the Trenton soupkitchen

Figure 4.5b. Painting in the Trenton soupkitchen

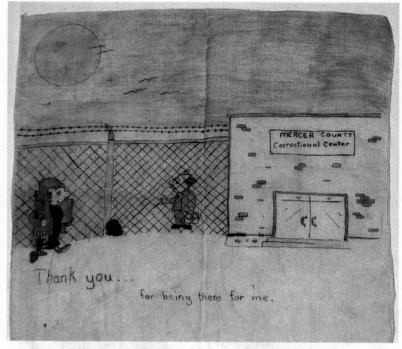

Figure 4.6. "Thank you ... for being there for me" (Trenton)

painting at the New York Outsider Art Fair. When Sally comes to collect
me, she points out the work of a woman who makes wonderful dolls, and
Alice shows me the work of a man who made it, in jail, out of unusual
materials like chewing gum wrappers[10].

As we drive back to Princeton, I reflect on the experience. It strikes me
that it was like participating in a work of art. Alas, however, this was not
a performance. It is the ugly reality of outsiders, the poor and marginalized of society, living in an atmosphere of oppression. Is there any hope
for these people? Sally tells me that for the clients of the soup kitchen

who participate in the art workshop, there is a sense that life can be different. They find, perhaps for the first time in their lives, that what they do is appreciated. While their art may not be great art, like that of many of the other artists discussed here, their flowers, their feathers, their colours are objects of beauty. It is like De Cruchy said: Ugliness and oppression are connected, and so are their opposites, beauty and redemption.

Haarlem: Voice in the City

In his book *Reikhalzend* (Yearning)[11], Jurjen Beumer, the pastor of *Stem in de stad* (Voice in the City), a group in the Dutch city of Haarlem, writes:

> "Recently we buried Henk, a frequent visitor to our Aanloopcentrum. Henk was one of the first guests of the drop-in center, about ten years ago. He died in the street close to his house. He had just left the center. As sad as we were, we told ourselves, 'He was lucky to die in the street, for how long would he have lain at home, all alone? We would not have missed him for some time.' Henk's greatest fear was to be all alone, to be dead and nobody would know. "Stay with me, stay with us, then too..." prayed the two from Emmaus (Luke 24:29). And we came to the service for Henk, everyone was there to say goodbye with a word, a poem, flowers. Many wept for Henk, for themselves, for the greatest loneliness. 'Stay with us' we prayed, 'for evening draws nigh and the day is almost over.'"

The passage is characteristic of Beumer's work in Haarlem. Most of the churches in that city participate in his Voice in the City project, in which they organize social activities to draw attention to the plight of the marginalized members of society, as well as cultural festivities. This is a prime example of the church of the future, in which the community interweaves elements of leitourgia and diakonia to create the "koinonia tou Christou".

Hospitality

In his dissertation on *Gastvrijheid* (Hospitality)[12], Sake Stoppels investigated the phenomenon of drop-in centers. In 1996 he counted over eighty such centers in the Netherlands, and suggested that the centers are "of interest within the broader framework of the church's presence in modern society". According to Stoppels, 'presence' has the meaning of 'God with us'. Writes Stoppels, "'Presence' has its source and inspiration in the God of Israel, He who is present. His presence is manifested in particular in Jesus Christ." At the same time, notes Stoppels, God is also ahead of us: "God's presence is not the result of the work of the church, but is, rather, the strong appeal to the church to be where He already is." Thus the concept of 'presence' emphasizes 'humanizing' rather than 'Christianizing'. Drop-in centers offer hospitality, which Stoppels calls "an essential aspect of the presence of the church". Although hospitality has primarily a secular meaning and does not occur much in the Bible, there are several important themes associated with it. One of these is what I call 'longing'. Stoppels notes that "the Lord preserves the strangers" (Psalm 146:9) and that Israel itself was a stranger in Egypt (Deuteronomium 10:19). Another is that of hospitality given unknowingly to God, as Abraham did in Genesis 18, or to Christ (Matthew 25:35). Hospitality also has an eschatological significance, in that one day all nations will go up to 'the mountain' (Isaiah 25), which is Jerusalem, and Christians believe that Jesus Christ will come back there and offer hospitality on the new earth under a new heaven.

The drop-in centers that Stoppels studied varied greatly, and he came up with eleven 'building blocks' with which to reflect on their role. The drop-in center is a community of 'non-equals' (1), but at the same time in many ways of 'equals' (2). The centers focus on the vitality and gifts of their guests rather than on their limitations and problems (3). Solidarity with these individuals goes hand in hand with the search for the transformation of society (4). Drop-in centers can be seen as salvific places where people can find and develop companionship, an earthly parallel to the community of saints (5). At the same time, the existence of unavoidable loneliness is recognized (6). Stoppels believes that drop-in centers should be part of a larger whole (7), though this is often not the case. For example, the center could place itself in the service of the Gospel (8), in which case the center should be expected to be a praying community (9),

and not a "passageway" (10) to the conventional church. As a manifestation of 'presence', therefore, the center needs to "find the right balance
between a maximum reserve in and a maximum readiness to invite the
other to form a personal alliance with the Eternal and to follow Christ"
(11).

Stoppels' building blocks are partly based on empirical observation,
but most of them have a normative aspect. Similarly, the discussion with
which he closes the study concerns the normative concept of 'sharing a
meal'. Stoppel notes that, like 'hospitality', 'sharing a meal' is doubly
rooted. First, the sharing of a meal and hospitality are inextricably connected in the world of the Old and New Testaments: the guest becomes
a table companion. Second, survey data have shown that the sharing of a
meal has become an increasingly important part of the functioning of
drop-in centres. In an era in which the family meal, eating together, is
threatened, the Christian community has good reason to try to maintain
(or rehabilitate) this custom, not least because the Christian community
is itself nourished by it. Moreover the Christian community, argues
Stoppels, is preparing itself for the great, eschatological Holy
Communion. In the open-table community, Christ's congregation follows Him, inviting people who otherwise would be excluded from the
circle to join them at the table.

Rotterdam: Pauluskerk

Reverend Visser is the pastor of a drop-in center at the Pauluskerk (St
Paul's Church) in Rotterdam. This drop-in center is probably the best
known such center in the Netherlands. This notoriety, even among the
general public and the media, is based on Visser's conflicts with the government in his struggle for the rights of drug addicts, especially prostitutes. His 'clients' are often violent, which does not endear them to the
public[13].

In his dissertation *Creativiteit, wegwijzing en dienstverlening* (Creativity,
guidance and service), Dr. Visser describes the role he attributes to the

church in the post-industial city. "The city and the place of the church in
it fascinate me", he writes. "My job in the Pauluskerk presented me with
opportunities to experiment with various modes of church functioning in
the city."[14] Elsewhere he wrote about the beginnings of his work in
Rotterdam, in 1979. "A short time after my arrival in Rotterdam I talked
with the municipal councillor for social affairs, Mrs. Schmitz, now the
mayor of Haarlem. I asked her what the council expects from subsidized
institutions like ours. She responded that officials must no longer try to
improve the world from behind their desks, but must go out in the street.
As the groups most urgently in need of help she mentioned migrants,
drugs users and prostitutes. Her strong emotional commitment to the
plight of the disadvantaged impressed me and I took her advice to heart. I
shifted my attention to the street."[15] Some time later, Visser encountered a
drug addict injecting himself next to the church.

> "I went to the boy and started talking to him. He accepted my invitation to
> come in and for the first time in my life I talked seriously with a heroin user.
> I remember he told me that the misery in his life started when his mother
> died. He did not get along with his stepmother. At that time I thought
> shooting up in dark corners disgusting".

Visser's next encounter with a drug user was with a woman who landed in
a hospital, where he visited her. A friend brought her drugs. She asks Visser
for money for tobacco and candy.

> "I brought her laundry to my wife, who was not very enthusiastic about the
> relationship, especially when she heard the woman tried to get money from
> me. Through painful experience I learned how to handle the manipulative
> actions of a drug user. One afternoon I refused to give her money. She made
> a scene and followed me to the doorway and even outside the hospital! She
> cried for money. 'That lousy church always leaves us in the lurch, how can
> you call yourself a minister when you let me down this way?' Help does not
> mean always doing what the other wants. One must make contracts. I will
> not force her to behave as I think good, and she will not force me to fulfil
> her demands. Once she phoned me late at night and begged for money.
> I refused. She answered, 'Then I'll have to turn tricks.' I replied, 'Do what
> you have to do. We made our contract, didn't we? There was silence on the
> other end of the line. Finally she said, 'You're right'."

Amsterdam/South Africa: AIDS

This attitude of acceptance – which means accepting the other for what he or she is, but does not necessarily imply an acceptance of the situation – is characteristic of many Dutch workers in the ministry of mercy and justice. One whose work in this area has been widely recognized is Greta Huis, who together with her collegue Ricus Dullaert worked for many years in the Roman Catholic pastoral ministry for drug users in Amsterdam. In his foreword to a book about Huis and Dullaert, the mayor of Amsterdam wrote: "City council makes political, financial, economic, social and cultural policy to ensure the welfare of citizens. We also provide programs and services for drug users. But the churches have their own unique approach, and it is invaluable. They know of the traumatic experiences that led drug users to do what they do. They encounter them as whole people, deserving of respect."[16]

Greta Huis' parents sold fruit and vegetables on the Fish Market in Groningen, where Greta often helped out. No doubt this environment contributed to developing her frank character and loud voice. After completing a journalism degree, Huis went on to study theology. This brought her into contact with the work of Dullaert, which was to change her life. While participating in training course at the Church of St. Mary in Harlem, New York, Huis made the decision to work with Dullaert in providing pastoral care to drug users in Amsterdam.

Dullaert, an antique dealer, lived in an elegant home in Amsterdam while working as a part-time pastor. A quiet man who inspires confidence in those around him, Dullaert accepts and respects the people with whom he works. He provides a rock-like presence to the constantly changing and often chaotic community of drug users. Drug addicts, always coping with the many uncertainties of their unstable life, are much in need of such a quiet and convincing person as Dullaert.

In a slum near Johannesburg, Dullaert now leads a team of welfare workers who minister to people infected with HIV during their last years or months. He listens and counsels. He looks both naïve and convincing as he says "come, let us pray", has a little talk with God, and recites the Lord's Prayer.[17]

Greta Huis was impressed by Dullaert's method of preaching. Instead of delivering a sermon, Dullaert tells a story from the Bible and develops a dialogue between it and the life and environment of his audience. At the last service he held in Amsterdam before leaving for South Africa, he spoke about his problem with God, wondering aloud why some people have all the luck while others always suffer misfortune.

Huis follows the same method. After telling a Bible story she asks two questions about the pericope. Soon, the discussion grows heated. Some of those present, tired and stoned, fall asleep, others listen silently, cigarette in hand. There are always people coming and going. Greta moderates the discussion from time to time, reminding her listeners that everyone should have a chance to voice their opinions. Surely there are not many church services in which the participants take the proclamation so strongly to heart as they do here. After the prayers, Greta asks for the blessing of God – Mystery, Mother and Friend – and the participants shake hands and wish each other the "Peace of Christ".

4.4. Presence: A Way of Social Attentiveness

In his theory of presence, Roman Catholic scholar Andries Baart distinguishes between the "Problem-solving" approach and the approach of "being present".

Social workers and other professional helpers like doctors make a diagnosis of problems troubling the life of their client and try to solve them as efficiently and conveniently as possible. The solution will generally be the result of a combination of the wishes of the client and the possibilities of the worker in a given situation. The worker intervenes professionally and withdraws as soon as the objective has been attained or, in many other cases, when the time and money allocated has been spent.

By contrast, pastors, "big brothers", volunteers at houses for the homeless and the like characteristically do not do a lot of problem-solving. Their function, primarily, is to give of themselves: to be there for the other, to listen, go for a walk or drink a cup of coffee, or assist in small jobs like shopping, accompanying somebody to a doctor's appointment or to visit a grave, perhaps to send wishes on an important anniversary. Another type of help is providing support in case of crime, violence and neighbourhood quarrels.

As Baart notes, this is not systematic, theory-directed problem-solving. It is certainly not what one would call a professional approach, though professionals as well as volunteers may work this way. Problems may be addressed, and may even be solved, but this is not the main point. What matters is the relationship, which can be successful even when problems are not solved[18]. In 2001 Baart published the results of a long- term research project on the subject of presence. The study is about two pastors in Utrecht who worked in severely socially and economically disadvantaged parts of the city. Most of the people they worked with felt "socially superfluous". In other words, they suffered not only from poverty, but even more from the sense that they themselves and their contribution to society were useless and not valued.

The method of 'presence' is an approach that is greatly appreciated by the people who see themselves as social outsiders. It is also costly, in that it requires a huge investment of time.

This neighbourhood-level pastoral work is characteristically done from the street, with neither permanent centers nor fixed strategies or agendas. Pastoral presence, writes Baart, "initially gets its form and content from more or less casual encounters, which are systematically expanded into long-term relationships based on trust and often extend to whole social systems like families or streets". These relationships, in a non-selective and unconditional way, merge with the lifeworlds, biographies and histories of the inhabitants, providing a space for people to articulate their pain, their longings, their needs. In terms of method, this kind of neighbourhood work demands a long-term, non-interventionist exposure to the life of the neighbourhood, and the development of a corresponding professional strategy. Key conditions are unhurriedness, unconditional attentiveness and receptivity. It takes a great deal of time and patience to win the confidence of the people one is working with, and then to coach them in coping with their existential questions and turning points during and through instrumental and gratuitous actions – by helping with a job or solving a practical problem, and by simply being present in a non-intervening way when there is something to celebrate, to mourn, to talk about. In many cases the workers simply participate in the everyday life of the inhabitants and deal with "superficial" issues, but certain expectations, roles and practices inevitable develop through which the pastoral worker attains a position of trust and, secondarily, can point the way to formal institutions. The deepest level is pastoral care concerning matters of personal identity, coping and life orientation.

Some of the experiences that the study examines were associated by the pastoral workers with Christian tradition and ritual. These were often associated with the wish of residents to be seen, to have a name, to be part of a larger community. Rituals such as eating together, be it at home, in a coffee shop or in a park, sharing food, be it a bag of potato chips, fruit or chewing gum, merit particular attention. One pastor recalls visiting a rape victim in her home. As the woman spoke to the pastor about her 'body and blood', she offered food and said, "Take, eat", and insisted, "Please, take, eat". The pastor was struck by the fact that in this setting, these significant words were at the same time the emotionally loaded request to "partake in my disfigured life, live on what I live on."[19]

To recover and maintain human dignity, and to offer or mobilize resources to this end are what Baart identifies as the first goal of "presence". "Exercizers of presence" are patient and focus on the good and interesting sides of a person rather than on problems and failures. They cannot alleviate suffering and need, but can make life bearable for those in need.

My wife, who is a pastor, recently told me about a woman who was very depressed, a condition made worse by the recent loss of her mother and the incurable illness of her father. The doctor had advised her to visit a psychotherapist but the woman, who had been there before, said to my wife, "I am too tired to try to think about how to solve my problems. Thank you for being there to listen to me. I need to talk about it, no more, no less". Presence.

4.5. Exposure

For professionals in the ministry of mercy and justice, a period of supervised "exposure training" is essential. "Exposure immerses pastors in a world that was previously unknown to them, in hopes that their prejudices will be overcome as they gain a more realistic understanding of the actual lived life in the neighbourhood".[20]

The two pastoral workers in Baart's study began their work with a period of several months in which they systematically walked through the neighbourhood in which they planned to work.

The worker does this at all times of the day and all days of the week, visiting snackbars, clubs and shops, looking around in parks, small streets and underpasses, in doorways and at bus shelters. She becomes conscious of the colours, of the cars, the dogs, the graffiti, the rubbish. She looks at the people, making an effort to hear them and to understand what they do and say. She may even talk to some of them. She keeps up a diary of everything that goes on outside and inside herself.

Another type of exposure, that takes place in an industrial setting, consists of a one- to three-month period of working with unskilled labourers and living with their families while receiving coaching from a team of experts.

Our students in Groningen, at the end of their studies for the church ministry, spend a week in the house of a marginalized member of society through Gerrit Jan van der Kolm's home for "outsiders" in Dordrecht, "to be confronted with the problematic of a district with cultural and social-economical problems, and to reflect on it." Such a short "exposure training" could also be organized in a hostel for the homeless, a centre for drug addicts, or a refugee centre.

In his study Baart found that the months of exposure are marked by several stages, beginning with disorientation and a need for self-control to avoid distantiating oneself from the estranging situation, a struggle to avoid thinking oneself superior to the people and the circumstances one encounters, and ending with a much enhanced receptivity to the newly discovered lifeworlds and visions of reality prevailing in the neighbourhood. Good supervision is essential to a successful outcome.

4.6. "AZC": State Refugee Centres and the Way Deacons Observe the Human Right to Live in Freedom

Across Europe, mostly in quiet, out-of-the-way places, a new kind of village is appearing. Resembling trailer parks, they are built to house four to eight hundred refugees from outside the European Union who seek political asylum.

These refugees, or asylum-seekers as they are known in Europe, are provided with the necessities of life: shelter, warmth, food and clothing. Yet they live an exhausting balancing act, poised between hope and fear. Their lives turn on whether their application for asylum will be accepted. About 80% of those seeking asylum will be returned to their countries of origin.

Like the Kulokovas from Chechnya. Travelling legally with Russian passports, they arrived in the Netherlands without a visa and requested asylum, thus launching their refugee determination procedure.[21] I am afraid they will have to return to Russia, for presumably they will not be persecuted.

Or like Mrs. Nazir from Afghanistan. When I met her in November 2001, the Taliban were still in control and therefore she and her husband had reasonably good chances of being granted a residence permit. Nevertheless, they were terribly anxious about family members who had remained behind and of whom they had had no news.

Refugees awaiting a decision on their fate enjoy many benefits. Children attend school, adults have opportunities to learn Dutch or English (figure 4.7) and to develop useful skills. They receive money for their own households, and are free to move about outside the centre. One thing they are not allowed to do – surprisingly, given the European work ethic – is to earn their own living. This was a curious discovery of the Brazilian artist Santiago Sierra, when he set out to stage a new version of an installation on the horrors of homelessness that he had originally mounted in Guatemala. Sierra invited poor people to earn some money by sitting in cardboard boxes for four hours a day. Inspired by the German debate on foreigners and asylum seekers in German society,

Figure 4.7. AZC Wolvega (NL), The First Exam

Sierra mounted a new version of the installation at the Kunst-Werke art show in Berlin in 2000.

For the project, volunteers – all foreigners from outside the EU seeking asylum in Germany – spend four hours a day sitting in cardboard boxes for the duration of the exhibition. In the narrow boxes, which are reminiscent of slum housing or shipping crates, it is impossible to move, let alone work. The boxes are closed, except for holes to let in air, so that the sitters are hidden from the viewer's sight.

The invisible physical presence, silent and immobile, is an alarming metaphor for the situation of asylum-seekers in Germany. On one hand they are invisible because they are housed in special centers and forced into inactivity because they are prohibited from working or travelling. On the other hand their concealment and isolation are in part voluntary because of the threat of assaults from neo-Nazies.

The title given to the German installation, *Six People Who Cannot Be Paid for Sitting in Cardboard Boxes*, relates to the specific situation of asylum seekers in Germany. When explaining his project to potential volunteers, Sierra realized that these people would not accept money for their participation because to take part in paid employment would jeopardize their legal situation. Since paying the sitters is normally an essential part of Sierra's work, the artist decided to allude to the specific German circumstances in the title.[22]

The state organizes and pays for the centers. However, there is much work to do for volunteers. Volunteers of the Dutch organization of Refugee Help provide legal aid; others assist or supervise the workers in the daycare center, the bar, or the shop; many volunteers give [Dutch] lessons for the adults. The churches can of course be part of this network of voluntary assistance. Like every volunteer, they must respect other religions, worldviews and political convictions. They are not allowed to discuss politics or religious issues.

A significant number of congregations offer help to refugees whose applications have been rejected but who have nowhere to go, given the intolerable situation in their country of origin. If they remain, they are legally non-persons, without the right to social or medical care of any kind. Thus a congregation may offer help to a refugee or family of refugees, though it is only a drop in the ocean. In the Oranjekerk in Amsterdam, for example, the congregation had to renovate their church and took the opportunity to create a small apartment for temporary guests that also can be used to house a refugee.

Governments must look after the interests of their citizens, keep order, and provide a strong economic foundation. They talk with the mouth of the voters[23]. Churches, especially church members involved in diakonia, have the freedom to observe in a different way than do democratically chosen governments, and must have the courage to do so. In the Netherlands, in April 2002, the Council of Churches presented a manifesto, *For a Human Existence*, to the parliament. They ask for a general pardon for those refugees, who are the victims of the negative effects of recent new European legislation about seeking asylum.

Churches need to speak the Word of God, as spoken by the prophets and by Jesus. They need to be concerned with mercy and justice for all, without distinction of citizenship, country of origin or legal status. Awoken by the Spirit, who plants the vision of goodness and righteousness in their hearts and minds, they have the freedom to look on the strangers in our midst as the Spirit looks on them: as God's creatures, and to offer them food, shelter, practical help and consolation.

CHAPTER 5.

AESTHETIC INSTALLATIONS

5.1. Dare to Observe! Examples in a Nutshell: Beuys, Acconci et al.

Dare to observe!

Dare to observe! This is the motto of this book, and it is especially pertinent when we look at the following examples of postmodern art. Sometimes we are not even able to observe what we see in reality. At the Whitney Museum of American Art in New York, I saw a work by Fred Sandhurst, *Untitled* (1987)[1], consisting of a large sheet of glass about two yards wide and six yards high, extending up to the ceiling. I thought it a little dangerous to place such a large sheet of clear, unprotected glass where people could walk into it. But when I looked again I saw that it was a trick of vision: not glass, but simply a black acrylic string, three millimeters thick, running from the ceiling to the floor, across the floor and up again on the other side. The string was installed very precisely, and the edges of the 'glass' were perfectly straight. I could look at the string as a sheet of glass, and then again I could see it as simply a piece of string. Another visitor layed his hand on the glass to demonstrate the joke to his children. Optical illusion can lead our vision completely astray, as Sandhurst illustrates in such masterly fashion. How much more attentive we must be to observe things we cannot even see 'at second sight': things hidden by 'the lying wing' as Schulze called it, injustices, things we prefer to forget. Perhaps, by observing and learning to understand postmodern art, we learn to observe and dare to expose ourselves to what is behind the lying wing.

World views

Few aesthetic installations will have as strong an impact on artists and visitors as those created as part of the summer 2001 *World Views* program. Since 1997, this program has provided young artists with the opportunity to work in a ready-made studio space for periods of six months, offering time for reflection, dialogue, and interaction with peers and arts professionals. The artists in the program had the chance to create new works in a truly extraordinary environment, for they had the whole, glass-enclosed 92nd floor of the north tower of the World Trade Center.

Of the 14 artists only one, Michael Richards, was at work in the space on the early morning of September 11, when he perished in the attacks. The brochure that was prepared for the World Views exhibition at the New Museum of Contemporary Art in New York notes that Richards had been working on a sculptural series entitled *Tuskeegee Airmen*, an homage to African-American pilots who were awarded over 150 Distinguished Flying Crosses during the course of WWII but were never honored. In particular, he was completing a sculpture of an airman riding a falling, burning meteor.[2]

Despite their shock, grief, and loss, the artists were determined to complete their residency cycle and share the ideas and projects they had been working on prior to September 11. According to the exhibition brochure, they were "challenged to recreate destroyed work, reconceptualize work previously in progress and create works within constraints of limited time and resources, and balance intellectual, moral, and ethical concerns in light of the disaster."

In some of the works on display the shock is visibly present. Geraldine Lau's *Information Retrieval* consists of a map of New York containing open spaces scattered across it, as if she had seen the city through the windows around the studio space: buildings, streets, water, but also emptiness, and probably Ground Zero as well.

Kara Hammond's pencil drawings certainly recall the attack, for among the buildings remaining in the area around the World Trade

Centre she drew a steep spire rising much higher than the buildings around it named *Cenotaph*, a monument to people buried elsewhere.

Laurie Halsey Brown created a large installation entitled *Between looking right (when remembering) and looking left (when creating)*, with a hoarse, emphatic voice incessantly repeating: "I am asking you a question"...

Some examples in a nutshell

Joseph Beuys, *Tramstop* (*Cleve*), monument for the future

In 1947, when the famous German artist Joseph Beuys was 26 years old he made, only a second-year student in art, a head which looks much like himself. This head has to do with another work of Beuys, an installation made for the Biennale in Venice in 1976.

The installation is an enriched remembrance of his youth in Cleve, his visits to an uncle in a nearby village. In those days Joseph often waited for the tram next to a remarkable signpost made in 1650 after the Thirty Years War from the remains of guns. As young Joseph waited there, he did not think about the brutality and futility of war, or about how instruments of war could be put to more peaceful uses. Rather, he dreamed of being a soldier, having adventures and travelling to faraway places. Later, Beuys served for four years as a pilot in the German air force, and these years profoundly affected him, making him into a man who observed human reality in a very critical way.

The installation fills a large room in the Cleve Kurhaus. It is made of tram rails, tram line switches, gun parts, and a structure resembling a signpost that ends in the head of a person crying (figure 5.1 and 5.2). The crying head could be a victim of war, but there is also a resemblance to the head of the young man Beuys created in 1947 (visible near a window on figure 5.2). The installation invites the viewer to recall, in his or her own way, the musing boy at the tram stop, the terror and futility of war, and the fact that despite the lessons of the past, human beings continue

Figure 5.1 Joseph Beuys, *Strassenbahnhaltestelle* (*Tramstop*).
Museum Kurhaus Kleve – Ewald Matare-Sammlung,
Dauerleihgabe des Kröller-Müller-Museums, Otterlo (NL).
Photoes: Annegret Gossens.

Figure 5.2. Joseph Beuys, *Strassenbahnhaltestelle* (*Tramstop*).
Museum Kurhaus Kleve – Ewald Matare-Sammlung,
Dauerleihgabe des Kröller-Müller-Museums, Otterlo (NL).
Photoes: Annegret Gossens.

to make war again and again. As I stood before it I saw an Afghan woman in a Dutch refugee centre who, though she had fled the Taliban, was anxious about the family members left behind and bitter about the strange western invaders. It makes you cry and it is difficult to stop crying.

Joseph Beuys, *7000 Oaks*

The streets around the Dia Center for the Arts in Chelsea, in New York City, are home to one of Beuys' long-term installations. This one consists of oaks, paired with a columnar basalt marker rising approximately four feet above the ground (figure 5.3). The project is one of the offsprings of Beuys' ecologically inspired initiative in Kassel. In 1982, the Dia Art Foundation provided the initial financing for Beuys' project of planting seven thousand oak trees in Kassel, the German city well known for the Documenta art exhibition held since 1955, from 1972 every five years. Beuys explained that his project as a way not only of contributing in practical terms to the natural environment but also of raising ecological awareness – an awareness that would only grow as the tree-planting continued over many years. Beuys hoped to go completely outside what people normally think of as art and to "make a symbolic start for my enterprise of regenerating the life of humankind within the body of society" and preparing a positive future.

"The planting of seven thousand oak trees is thus only a symbolic beginning. And such a symbolic beginning requires a marker, in this instance a basalt column. The intention of such a tree-planting event is to point to the transformation of all life, of society, and of the whole ecological system."

"My point with these seven thousand trees was that each would be a monument, consisting of a living part, the live tree, changing all the time, and a crystalline mass, maintaining its shape, size, and weight. This stone can be transformed only by taking from it, when a piece splinters off, say, never by growing. By placing these two objects side by side, the proportionality of the monument's two parts will never be the same. So now we have six- and seven-year-old oaks, and the stone dominates them. In a

Figure 5.3. Joseph Beuys, *7000 Oaks* (here: the New York version)

few years' time we may see that gradually, the stone has become an adjunct at the foot of the oak…"

Beuys died early in 1986, but in June 1987, at the opening of Documenta VIII in Kassel, his son planted the last tree. Other projects in the same line followed. For Beuys intended the project to be only the first stage in an ongoing scheme of tree planting to be extended throughout the world.

Thus the 7000 Oaks function as inspirational images, embodying Beuys' "utopian and poetic metaphysic of a social sculpture designed to effect a revolution in human consciousness, 'the human being as a spiritual being'"[3].

Vito Acconci, *Other Voices for a Second Sight* (*1974*)

Acconci's work, created in the seventies, is called conceptual art. This kind of art emphasized ideas or concepts instead of the traditional art object. Acconci, who preferred a "lowtech performative style"[4], created his works in what he called an 'isolation chamber', basically only for himself. He was interested in the immediacy of video. Able to see himself on the monitor as he was recording, Acconci plays with his own body. The work I saw at the Whitney Museum of American Art is a three-room video installation combining psychological explorations of personal identity with a broader political theme, "a pastiche of communiques from revolutionaries such as Che Guevara (…), articulating the loss of direction and integrity that he and other artists felt had taken place during the Vietnam era." "Acconci's identity is split between these three rooms, and, within them, further split into fragments of meandering narrative in which he occupies multiple identities searching for a stable place in which to lodge the self.[5]"

In this overwhelmingly complex work, Acconci shows the changes of mind and identity that result from growing doubt about the desirability of the continuous progress of modernity. These doubts were already expressed in Pop and Minimalist Art, but the collapse of traditional personal and political values was accelerated by the loss of the Vietnam War and the oil crisis, both in 1973. Postmodern philosophy and art were the first to recognize the fragmentation of identity. Acconci's *Other Voices for a Second Sight* is an excellent example of how artists are often forerunners in observing changes in human identity and future politics. Even thirty years after it was created, his work is an eye-opener.

David Wojnarowicz, *What's This Little Guy's Job in the World?*

In David Wojnarowicz's show, winter 1998, in the New Museum of Contemporary Art on Broadway, entitled Fever, I was, in particular, struck by the photograph of the baby frog in the palm of the artist's hand, entitled *What's This Little Guy's Job in the World?*, with the following text in the corner:

> "What is this little guy's job in the world. If this little guy dies does the world know? Does the world feel this? Does something get displaced? If this little guy dies does the world get a little lighter? Does the planet rotate a little faster? If this little guy dies, without his body to shift the currents of air, does the air flow perceptibly faster? What shifts if this little guy dies? Do people speak language a little bit differently? If this little guy dies does some little kid somewhere wake up with a bad dream? Does an almost imperceptible link in the chain snap? Will civilization stumble?"

Wojnarowicz's biography helps us to understand his work. He died of AIDS in 1992 at the age of 37. A victim of abuse during his childhood in Red Bank, New Jersey, he turned to prostitution and by the age of 16 was living on the street. In the late 1970s he began working in various artistic media: first photography, later on painting, sculpture, and performance art. In 1988, when he discovered his HIV status, he embarked on a fierce critique of American politics and way of life. He began dealing with his impending death and his ongoing battle with AIDS, is also the theme of *What's This Little Guy's Job in the World?*, dating from 1990.

Nedko Solakov, *A life (Black and White)*

In January 2002, while visiting New York's PS1. Contemporary Art Center, now part of MoMA, I saw a show about time called Loop, alluding to the recyclability of time and the repetition of historical time, but also to the time, often useless, that is spent at leisure and work. "Time appears to be tangible and serviceable, a phenomenon capable of being influenced, lengthened or repeated. (...) Two video works by artists from a previous generation, Bruce Nauman and Marina Abramovic, point to the tradition in which the works of the younger artists are set. Using the potential of the most modern media technology, these artists give visual form to philosophical questions, which involves dividing time up into small sections and holding it up as if in a loop, by continual repetition of the same process. Continuous return keeps everything in an agitated stillness, which leads nowhere and which raises the question of life's purpose."[6] People can live longer and longer, but for what? Life is recyclable, as in the myth of Sisyphus.

This theme is another example of the potential of art to widen our outlook. Here, our view on time with respect to our understanding of human feelings of a meaningless life, which can lead to despair, social isolation and solitude.

Slovenian artist Nedko Solakov created an unusual performance on this theme: *A Life (Black and White)* (figure 5.4a and 4b). For the duration of the show, two employees of the museum paint the walls of a room, one with black paint, the other with white. Each continually follows the other, without either one ever achieving their goal. In this way Solakov demonstrates the tragedy of eternal return, the myth of Sisyphus as an image of time.

Carola Dertnig, *Revolving Door*

Dertnig, one of the World Views group of young artists, lives and works between Vienna and New York. Her intriguing and humorous video project shows the artist, laden with packages and pushing an empty stroller, trying to pass through a small revolving door. The social criticism contained in many of Dertnig's works is implicit here in the range of reactions of bystanders. Most people pay little attention and get out of the way as quickly as they can, while some are clearly annoyed as they

Figure 5.4a Solakov, *A life (Black and White)*

Figure 5.4b. Solakov, *A life (Black and White)*

wait impatiently to get through the door themselves. Others simply wait quietly. Just as it looks as if she is about to negotiate the door successfully, she turns the wrong way, as if trapped. Several people behind her take advantage of this opportunity to go through the door. But some – only a few – try to help her escape from the seemingly endless circle.

Jorge Pardo & Gilberto Zorio, *Reverb*

Reverb, an installation by the Cubane-American artist Pardo and the Italian artist Zoria at the Dia Center for the Arts in 2001, is a combination of Pardo's design for the ground floor of the Dia Center, and an older work by Zorio. The subject of boundaries has occupied Zorio since the sixties. "A boundary is an imagined line, which becomes concrete through violence", he maintains. "The concept of a boundary carries multiple meanings. When it takes concrete material existence, it impacts decisively, aggressively – in short, violently – upon its surroundings: when immaterial, abstract, or invisible, it may be a dividing line between states, a restriction on the self." In *Microfoni*, Zorio placed microphones inside a rather small space. Visitors could speak into the microphones, making audible contact across boundaries that were closed to the eye. Thirty years after *Microfoni* was last presented, Zorio was invited to recreate the work within Pardo's indelible redesign of Dia's ground floor. At the same time Pardo was also invited to respond to this proposal. Zorio freely reconfigured his pioneering work, while Pardo made a trio of interconnecting parts of the Dia space, using curtains in the original orange-red-yellow colours of the floor. Zorio installed microphones in various corners of the three parts, by which visitors can talk and be heard in every corner of Pardo's project, thus again crossing boundaries, this time the curtained-off spaces.

The curator of the show notes that "*Reverb* echoes the present cultural climate, marked as it is by an unprecedented level of exchange and engagement between artists from very different generations, circumstances, and aesthetics"[7]

In his work, Zorio opens closed boundaries so that violence may be stopped and people from different nations and cultures can learn from each other – perhaps share in each others spiritual and material richness or, at least, learn to live together in peace.

5.2. An Elaborate Example: Mathilde ter Heijne, *Life Inside Storage*

Since 1998, Mathilde ter Heijne has made several installations consisting of heaps of cardboard boxes bearing stamps indicating place of origin, shipping routes, weight, contents and so on. In an introduction to another version, Ter Heijne's work *Displaced Delivery*, it is said that "traditionally, frame structures are used in an exhibition to support, protect and draw attention to a work of art or to isolate the site or object to be inspected. Unlike frames, Ter Heijne's box structures enclose and surround images but they do not isolate a visual detail or add value to its contents. Rather the constructions are attempts to distinguish one item from another and become carriers of ambiguous messages."[8]

Life Inside Storage (figure 5.5, 5.6 and 5.7) is about a similar estrangement. It consists of the same cardboard boxes, containing goods of various kinds from all over the world, boxes that are unrelated, fragmented, unidentifiable and anonymous – abstract as it were. As in *Displaced Delivery*, holes cut into the side of several boxes are fitted with plastic lenses that distort what is inside. Behind the lenses Ter Heijne has placed photos or collages of different scenes representing social ills and collective human misery. It is her intention to show what we all do: abstracting and packaging the suffering of mankind.

Paradoxically, she makes what Gerhard Schulze called the 'lying wing' visible in a hidden way.

Looking at this work in terms of the theories, explicated in Chapter 1, of Dickie, Danto, Cauquelin, Seel and Welsch, as well as my own approach, we can come to some tentative conclusions.

According to Dickie, we might formulate the following aesthetic and cognitive syllogisms:

Figure 5.5. Mathilde ter Heijne, *Life inside storage*

Unity in a work of art is always valuable. *Life inside storage* is unified. Therefore it is valuable, that is, has some degree of good in it.

Intensity, the aura emanating from a work of art, is always valuable. *Life inside storage* has some intensity. Therefore it also has some value in this respect.

Complexity means that a work of art is not univocal, but consists of many elements. *Life inside storage* shows complexity. Therefore it is valuable, that is, has some degree of good in it.

Elegance means that a work of art is refined or decorative. *Life inside storage* is elegant in some of its details. Therefore it is valuable, that is, has some degree of good in it.

Truth to actuality in a work of art is always valuable. *Life inside storage* is in many ways true to actuality. Therefore it is valuable, that is, has some degree of good in it.

Dickie would surely praise Ter Heijne's work, based on his criteria for evaluating art.

Danto asks about the conceptual complexity, the purpose and the means of the work. I expect that he would concur with Dickie's judgment [as inferred by me], and approve of Ter Heijne's work. However, Dickie and Danto might have some problems with the almost explicit moral meaning of Ter Heijne's work.

According to Seel's method of judging by a process of argumentaton, the moral connotations of *Life inside storage* would doubtless be approved, for though almost visible, they are actually part of the metaphor shown in the work.

Cauquelin's assessment starts with 'disinterestedness', though always with regard to the viewer's frame of reference; we also need to be educated about the artwork, and prove whether it is 'unique', original, or filled with new meaning. The final moment, according to Cauquelin's theory, is that of "communiquer", which has to do with all of the former ones. Moral or discursive activities are part of the game, and the outcome must be that the work of art is not informative but educating, which is true of *Life inside storage*.

Welsch's theory of judging the value of works of art is not unlike Cauquelin's and my own. Welsch ends his critique with an overall

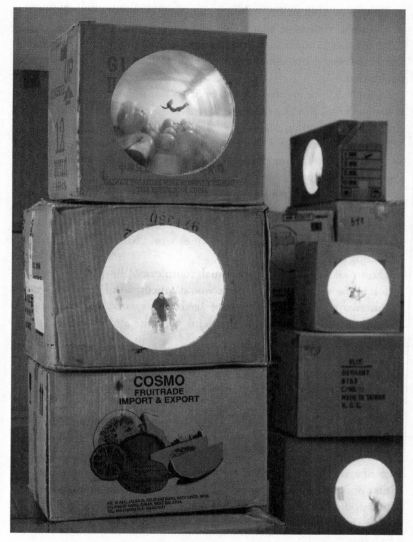

Figure 5.6. Mathilde ter Heijne, *Life inside storage* (part of the installation)

view of the area of the phenomenon, which often results in critical ethical remarks. He too would accept the artistic quality of Ter Heijne's work.

When my wife saw the boxes and identified the pictures, she remarked spontaneously: "This is really a learning project on diakonia, an eye-opener." I agreed, though we had to go back and look at the installation again to understand what we had intuitively felt the first time we saw it. Here we have a good example of the three phases of observing and understanding a work of art. We immediately felt the impact of the installation (phase 1a), but had to spend more time working out the meaning for ourselves (phase 1b). Rabinowitz's sophisticated commentary on the working of the disordered and unrelated heap of cardboard boxes from all over the world added a new depth to our understanding. We realized that the form of the work was a way of abstracting human suffering. We see it at a distance and we know: "There is so much war and hunger and pain, it is everywhere in the world the same mess, we cannot help it."

But as soon as we draw closer to the boxes, and especially when we start observing one specific image, we are existentially moved by the scene of suffering.

As a result of the preceding steps, we understand much better how the installation works and how it affects us (phase 3). Most of the time we see suffering from a distance and avoid dealing with it. We distance ourselves from suffering as a way of protecting ourselves from being overwhelmed by the endless need that exists in the world. The alienating effect of the cardboard box creates distance, presents us with an abstraction of evil and suffering, shields us from it. But as we move closer and look through the plastic lenses, we make contact with the details of suffering. If we allow ourselves to remain, to be exposed to the images and truly observe them, we experience the concrete nature of suffering and are personally moved. The choice is ours: to open our eyes and expose ourselves to what is in the box, or to turn our backs.

I had still another idea, which also can become an objection. "Look at the boxes with their superscriptions of countries of origin and destination

Figure 5.7. Mathilde ter Heijne, *Life inside storage* (detail)

and of the contents. How pleased we are to receive those boxes, full of things we desire, produced in countries with low wages. But the people who made and send the products, often in bad circumstances, we don't want to meet at all." The objection against this criticism looks like this: "Please let them stay home: The Netherlands for the Dutch people! Let them put things in order in their own countries, full of misery. Did not Ter Heijne show it to us?"

Very curious! We enter a room in a museum and see boxes. Looking more carefully we see nice pictures with pretty colours. But only if we really observe the pictures, we see the distress.

What about this heap of cardboard boxes?! In a project on diakonia we can use Ter Heijne's shocking installation as a real eye-opener.

5.3. Experiencing Aesthetic Installations

As the examples show, the observation of works of art can lead to "welt-bildende Erfahrungen", experiences that form our worldview. The observation may produce an immediate, intuitive understanding that corresponds to phase 1 of the three phases discussed in the first chapter. This is what happened to my wife and me when we saw Ter Heijne's work Life Inside Storage. Simply by looking at the work with an attitude of 'open observation' we experienced at once the reality of injustice and pain. In this case phase 3, comprehension, or the capacity to transfer the understanding of the work to other contexts, followed directly on phase 1. Phase 2, explanation, might have been interesting, but here no explanation was necessary in order to grasp, to transfer and to transform the meaning of this work.

By comparison, for Beuys' Tramstop, as well as for 7000 Oaks, I needed an explanation, a critical analysis, before I could transfer his message and imagine parallels to the emotions Beuys expressed. The experiences that Beuys described helped to clarify and reveal my own hidden and sometimes contradictory feelings about unjustice and suffering. Similarly, reading about the background of 7000 Oaks made me more aware of the struggle in myself between the desire for thoughtless consumption and the wish to make a better world.

David Wojnarowicz's show, *Fever*, also forced me to look deeply at my own internal conflicts and ambiguities. In particular, I was struck by the photograph of the baby frog in the palm of the artist's hand, entitled *What's This Little Guy's Job in the World?* In the case of this work, phase 1 (intuitive understanding) and phase 2 (critical analysis) go hand in hand. While the picture and the text are meaningful on their own, it is certainly helpful to know something of Wojnarowicz's biography to gain a fuller appreciation of the work.

The Poetry Summer of Watoe

Every summer for the past 21 years, in the Flemish village of Watoe has held a poetry festival that brings together poets and other artists to present contemporary poetry and visual arts, and create new connections between the art forms. Poems are projected onto large screens or shown on video amongst sculptures and installations.

I have not seen this exhibition, but here the comments of one Dutch critic, Henk Boon, writing about the work of Maja Bajevic of Sarajevo, offer insight into the phenomenon of observing, here Boon's way of observing[9]. He notes that Bajevic's installation consists of bunches of freshly cut reeds, laundry hanging on an old-fashioned line, and a tree stump suspended upside down from the ceiling of the barn in which the piece is housed. "The visitor must use a great deal of imaginative power to perceive in the situation presented by the artist something more than a symbol of gloom. The sense of gloom is heightened by our awareness that Bajevic still lives in Sarajevo, a place full of individual and collective trauma. A more successful piece is a work of ..."

Boon looks at a work of art and sets down an impression of it, including his emotional response. The reader can imagine and accept his suggestion of gloominess. Meanwhile, however, the critic supposes that the artist had in mind something deeper, perhaps metaphorical, that constitutes her 'real' message, but that she succeeded in conveying to viewers only a sensation of gloom, and that hence the work of art was not successful.

This critique is a good example of the variety of opinions in contemporary art criticism about what constitutes a successful work of art.

Boon sees simple, commonplace things in a new and unusual setting, but the experience does produce in his mind what Danto referred to as the transfiguration of the commonplace; the commonplace things are "gloomy" and he makes a judgement that this is not a successful work of art.

If one were to approach this work using the three-phase model, phase 1 – observation and intuitive understanding – and phase 2, critical analysis and knowledge of the artist's background and context, one might have the same emotional impression as Boon but reach quite a different conclusion – phase 3, renewed comprehension – about the value of the work.

Dickie, whose aesthetic theory was discussed in Chapter 1, judges the "instrumental goodness" of a work of art by its ability to produce valuable experiences. What kind of experiences could Bajevic's work produce that would be "valuable experiences"? Based on Dickie's model, we might formulate the following aesthetic and cognitive syllogisms: Unity in a work of art is always valuable. Bajevic's work is unified. Therefore it is valuable, that is, has some degree of good in it. Intensity, the aura emanating from a work of art, is always valuable. This work, obviously, has little intensity. Therefore, it is not valuable in this regard. Complexity means that a work of art is not univocal, but consists of many elements. This work shows little complexity. Therefore it is not valuable in this regard. Elegance means that a work of art is refined or decorative. This work is not elegant. Therefore it is not valuable in this regard. Truth to actuality in a work of art is always valuable. This work is true to actuality in some respects. Therefore it is valuable, that is, has some degree of good in it. In Dickie's eyes the work of Bajevic is only valuable, that is, has some degree of good in it, in certain respects. Thus, based on his critical analysis, and Dickie only uses phase 2, he would be unlikely to regard Bajevic's work as a successful work of art. Boon, who refers explicitly to phase 1 and implicitly to phase3, reaches the same conclusion about the value of the work.

Quite a different approach to judging the success of works of art was developed by the German critic Martin Seel[10]. In aesthetics, Seel argues, we discuss aesthetic understanding. A work of art is successful when we can find arguments for the truthfulness of the work. And the truth of aesthetic speech acts about a certain work of art depends on whether we can give good reasons for the 'world-transforming' powers of that work of art. Simply put, a work of art is successful if critics agree that it inspires in us feelings of beauty, goodness, justice and other positive ethical values.

Applying Seel's theory of the success of a work of art to the role of art in raising awareness of diakonia, one could say that when a work of art reminds people of goodness and righteousness that God wants us to live by in this world, it is successful and can be useful tool for consciousness-raising in diakonia.

From this point of view Balevic's could be considered successful, albeit subject to a number of conditions. As we observe it, we need to be aware of the traumatic situation in the artist's native city, and translate its gloominess into situations with which we are familiar. This process of observing and understanding a work of art, studying its background and context and ultimately gaining a renewed comprehension of the work as well as of its implications for the just and good life, can be a valuable tool in the process of learning regarding diakonia.

5.4. Awareness of Diakonia and Aesthetic Installations

In Chapter 2 I tried to explain how the process of creating a ritual, a performance or an installation on a particular subject can help us to gain a much deeper and more compassionate understanding of the subject.

Rituals, installations and performances are useful in schools as well as in educational programs about diakonia for adults because they can represent God's longing and hence, through the working of the Holy Spirit, the human longing to make something good of creation. The Holy Spirit kindles in us the desire to realize the Kingdom of God by bringing goodness and mercy to all. By making us observant of our own functions, needs and yearnings, the Spirit allows us to become aware of the needs of others, and therefore, as I have pointed out in Chapter 3, the "souci de soi", or care for oneself, is the basis for a socially caring mentality. What we want and feel in our innermost being, often without conscious awareness, corresponds to the wishes and feelings of others, and our suffering and needs give us a way of understanding of the suffering and needs of others.

The following installations are examples of works that may serve as the basis for projects or lessons designed to raise awareness of diakonia, in line with the theory presented in Chapter 2.5. In each case, the artist's original concept is retained, but the content may be adapted by the participants to represent particular diaconal issues or ideas.

The Box

This example occurred to me during a visit to an exhibition of the work of Dutch artist Michiel Huisman at the Stedelijk Museum in Amsterdam. This particular work is a very simple little wooden box fixed to the wall, with a button and a hole through which one can peep into the interior. When approaching the box, one hears loud pop music. But when one presses the button, the music changes to a soft classical tune and the interior lights up. Peeping through the hole one can see two birds wearing party hats in a decorated room. But one of the birds is huddled up, its hat askew, a picture of misery. The other bird tries to cheer it up by giving it a friendly tap on the shoulder. But the first bird remains sad amid the garlands and the beautiful music. As long as the viewer keeps pressing the button, the light inside the box remains on and the classical music plays. But as soon as one stops pressing, the box goes dark and the loud pop music resumes.

The change in the music immediately made me think of how Huisman's concept could be adapted to quite a different setting. In the interior of the box the viewer sees a sad or shocking story; the music inside is mournful or distraught rather than cheerful and sweet (figure 5.8). As soon as one stops pressing the button, the light goes off and loud music is all around. The beat, the rock, the rap goes on.

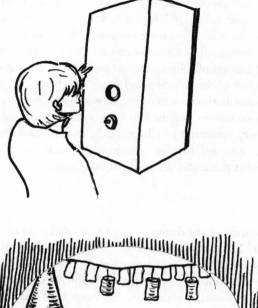

Figure 5.8. After Michiel Huisman, *The Box*

A Paradox

At an exhibition of Brazilian art at the Guggenheim Museum, I saw a curious installation by Regina Silveira entitled The Saint's Paradox. On a pedestal about six feet high, Silveira had placed a very small, gnome-like figure of wood, representing Saint James the Apostle. Though less than seven inches high, it casts a huge shadow on the two walls on either side. The shadow was that of a military hero whose statue stands in the center of Sao Paulo, at least thirty times the size of the little wooden figure.

Silveira's installation would help students or churchmembers studiing a project on diakonia. Some information would have to be provided, for example whom the wooden figure and the shadow are meant to represent, but no doubt a wide range of interpretations would be given. The group can use the work as a model for its own installations on various subjects with regard to the ministry of mercy and justice.

Other examples I gave in Chapters 2 and 3. In the last chapter I will describe a group that worked in a similar way.

CHAPTER 6.

THE COURAGE TO OBSERVE
*The Importance of Performance and
Installation Art for Christian Education
and its Tasks of Expanding Social Concern
and Outreach in the Congregation*

6.1. The Basis

In this last chapter I will try to make clear how the previous chapters form the basis for my wish to show the educational importance of art works, like performances and installations, for the growth of consciousness, with regard to diakonia, in the congregation.

In Chapter 1 I said that I feel at home with those (post-)modern artists whose work expresses something like the "transcendence of common beliefs". Behind the immanent commonplace, which is usually not difficult to express, there is more: the invisible. To express this demands a different kind of creative act: art as the revelation of the invisible.

I give another example. At the Documenta art fair in Kassel, Germany, I saw a piece by Austrian artist Lois Weinberger, composed of small, familiar plants and large, unfamiliar ones growing between the rails of a partly dismantled railway. Weinberger had planted neophyte exotic species between the plants that were already growing there. The commonplace was indicated, and transcended. As the artist pointed out, *Exotic seeds will soon overgrow the indigenous seeds.* To this common-sense description of the truly postmodern installation we could add an invisible message such as "Protect our wonderful alpine flowers!" But I had a worse idea; I suspected the artist of a hidden xenophobia, of using this installation to send a message about keeping foreigners out. Or perhaps the artist had a more positive motive?

"See those beautiful exotic flowers, it is a good thing they are stronger than the native ones!"

I did not need an explanation (phase 2) for I could distinguish two layers on my own: 'protect indigenous plants', and 'autochthones first!'. But to understand what the artist had in mind I needed the guide, which informed me that Weinberger has a deep interest in native plants, not only in Austria, but all over Europe. Showing this interest is the common-sense layer of his work. But the guide also informs us that the piece is "a vegetal metaphor for the migratory problems of our day, rooted in the artist's sense of black humor."[1]

What I learned from the guide about the installation, in other words in phase 2, was that the artist himself is the opposite of a fascist, and thus my deeper comprehension of the work (phase 3) was based on a fuller understanding of the artist himself.

Each work of art has, of course, an immanent origin. Many works of art, like Weinberger's, have a highly metaphorical and even transcendent character. It is evident from these works that the modern metaphors hidden in art can refer back to the immanent origin of the work in everyday life. Of course, for the work to remain a work of art, this referring back is not articulated by the work itself. Weinberger leaves it to the viewer to comprehend the meaning of his work for everyday life. Thus visitors and critics understand (1) and explain (2) the work – culminating, through the process of what Cauquelin calls "communiquer", in a deeper comprehension (3) of the metaphor and what it means for their worldview and actions in everyday life, so back to the immanent origin.

The same can be said about religious narratives and performances, such as rituals. Christians, as I have remarked, see in the person of Jesus a metaphor for the everyday figure of God. In liturgy, as in a work of art, we will not refer back to the immanent origin in everyday life. We say: "Jesus was a human being (the immanent origin), and in his human deeds he showed how God would act if God were a human being." In liturgy, however, we would be unlikely to follow this with: "So you must do this and that to live like Jesus", since to do so would be to detract from the power of the ritual and start moralizing. But as soon as we "communiquer", explain, this metaphor a little bit in a sermon, and out loud in teaching/learning processes, and if we 'live' this metaphor, e.g. by performing righteous acts, the ritual is fulfilled, as we demonstrate by our actions that our worldview and our actions have changed.

In this sense it can be said that aesthetic as well as religious experiences may be world-transforming, in a moral sense. Such experiences point upwards, but are located in the middle of everyday life.

In Chapter 2 we discussed the notion of longing, seen as the secular base of hope for goodness and righteousness. Christians will call this longing for the Kingdom of God, that is awakened in us by the Holy Spirit. 'Longing' is parallel to 'faith'. Both are gifts from God, but both must be brought to awareness through the tradition of the Christian culture. Though longing and faith are both 'grace', we can grow in longing and in faith. Longing for the Kingdom needs to be developed, and therefore we must 'dare to observe' reality with the eyes of Christ. This way of subjective aisthesis, observation, can be fostered by aesthetic and religious means. Always, however, the observer's frame of reference plays a crucial role in this process of observing. At first sight we only see that which we recognize and that on which we are able to focus. Our frame of reference is therefore shaped by our material and immaterial personal needs.

In Chapter 3 we argue, that the process of learning to observe need and fostering consciousness with regard to diakonia in the congregation is based on five steps. They are: being conscious of the present situation and context of the congregation with respect to diakonia; finding connections between the current situation and the biblical teachings about diaconate; focussing on the group to be helped by the deacons and their cooperators themselves; setting the congregation's policy and carrying it out. Every congregation can become more involved in the ministry of mercy and justice through working groups, 'para-communities' closely tied to the congregation and consisting of people dedicated to particular kinds of activities about diakonia.

So the best way to learn to 'observe need', is of course the direct experience of persons in situations of need and distress. But in order to encourage as many people, and specifically as many church members as possible to develop this awareness, even when they are not exposed to an acute situation of need, we can create learning opportunities as part of the education and teaching/learning processes of the church. Charity, compassion and sense of righteousness ought to be the second nature of Christians at church, at home and in their daily lives. For Christians believe that their own material and immaterial basic needs are created not only so that they can use their mental and physical skills to fulfil their own "souci de soi", their own egocentric longing for the just and good life, but also as a way of enabling them to understand and feel – to empathize with – the needs of other human beings. To bring attention to the love of God (leitourgia) and the love of one's neighbour (diakonia), they start from their own individual needs and wishes, but try to transfigurate the personal perspective into a wider horizon. This empathy can be taught and learned through rituals, bibliodrama and aesthetic performances and installations, which act as an opportunity to observe need and respond to it without being exposed to the direct experience.

Chapter 4 presented some examples of situations that invite us to observe or even to be exposed to circumstances that could lead to projects regarding diakonia. These situations have in fact inspired others to enter the ministry of mercy and justice, and to undertake projects aimed at helping people suffering from material need and other, less tangible ills. We only become aware of the open or secret religious and aesthetical messages about righteousness and the good life if we have learned to combine these messages with some of the insights from projects concerning diakonia.

Chapter 5 discusses how exposure to both works of art and to situations of suffering and need can deepen our insight into the importance of diaconate. In the following section we will look at an example of a teaching/learning process in the church about diakonia that makes use of the deeper comprehension obtained in this way.

6.2. Using Performances and Installations to Further Consciousness regarding Diakonia: Study Group "k.o.9", Autumn 2001

The course

In the autumn of 2001, a group of ten students aged 25 to 55, preparing for the ministry in our church, all in their sixth and last year of theological study, participated in a small project to further their consciousness with respect to diakonia. As we have seen in the preceding chapters, this can be done in a theoretical way or by being confronted directly with social need ('exposure'), or it can be done by a combination of the two approaches, resulting in some kind of evaluation. I proposed to the group members that, as suggested in this book, we use performances or installations to end such a project, and they agreed.

Our aim was that at the end of the course the students would be better prepared to understand and empathize with the problems, needs and feelings of individuals or groups in a specific situation of suffering. The whole project consisted of 40 hours of preparation spread over a span of three months. We used the three phases of Ricoeur and phase 4, implementation. The project took place as follows:

a. Before the first meeting the students had already thought about the subject of the project they wanted to focus on. At the first meeting I gave a lecture on the material contained in Chapters 1 and 2 of this book, and we discussed the projects the students wanted to share with each other. Several ideas for projects are discussed in Chapter 4. The students formed three groups and chose the projects "solitude in the church", "awareness of solitude" and "drop-in center". The students could also choose either to carry out direct, practical observation or to acquire knowledge indirectly through books, television programs or other sources about the subject. The two groups working on solitude chose the indirect approach; the third group visited drop-in centers and spoke to volunteers and visitors. Everyone was asked, over the course of the next three months, to make notes about feelings, observations, bright ideas or other thoughts having to do with the project. They were also asked to write down what they thought about their project at the beginning of the assignment and again at the end.

b. At the next session I offered a range of possibilities for how they might use their new knowledge, their direct or indirect observations, for a performance, to present the ideas of the group to the rest of the students. These possibilities are discussed in Chapter 5.

c. The remaining 30 hours or so were spent on observation (still phase 1), on group discussions (phase 2) and on preparing the performance or installation (phase 3). Although 30 hours is a relatively short time for such a project, they made the most of the time available to them.

d. One morning was dedicated to the actual performances (phase 4), which are described in detail in the next section.

e. After the performances the students were asked the following questions:

1. What did you think/feel before the course about the subject chosen by your group?

2. What did you think/feel before the course about possibilities for action with regard to the subject?

3. What did you learn from your fellow students about question 1 (their thoughts/feelings about the subject)?

4. What did you learn from your fellow students about question 2 (their thoughts/ feelings about possibilities for action with regard to the subject)?

5. What did you learn from the ideas and suggestions of your fellow students about the possibilities of making a performance or an installation on the subject?

6. Did this course change your thoughts/feelings about the subject (question 1 and 2), and if so how?

The performances

"Call me....I AM present" – Solitude in the church

The first group discussed the idea of fellowship in a congregation and its counterpart, feeling alone in what is called a community of faith. All of them realized immediately that the feeling of solitude is widespread not only in our society but also in our congregations. They pointed out that although the problem is well known, it is seldom addressed. What are the causes and types of loneliness in the congregation, and what kind of performance could be created to help members develop an awareness and understanding of the problem?

The group made a video showing both community and aloneness. There were shots of members of a congregation sitting in the pews of the church; older white people, very much at home and evidently involved in the church experience, and among them a black child, looking uneasy, looking left out and alone.

> "Who calls me, who takes care of me?
> Who asks for my name?
> Without being heard
> I cannot live."

These words, spoken at the beginning of the video, make it clear that consciousness regarding diakonia starts in the congregation. Are we focussing on the ideas and feelings of comfort of a particular group of members and ensuring their comfort, or are we looking around us, observing what is really going on in the congregation? The initial image of loneliness in the church signifies that we often are not aware of the real need, often unbearable, of many of the members of the congregation. The loneliness of elderly people is one such need with which we may be familiar.

The video showed many other examples, like the feelings one can have in a service, while surrounded by other people. For example, persons may be overcome with sadness or pain during a prayer on a theme that is currently affecting their life. A couple that has been unable to have children may be overcome by emotion during a baptism. A person who cannot find a partner may suffer great emotional distress during a wedding service. Homosexuals, alone or as a couple, often feel excluded from ordinary conversations about weddings, family or children that others take for granted.

> "Who calls me, who takes care of me?
> Who asks my name?
> Without being heard
> I cannot live
> and without an answer
> I cannot feel human.
> Alone,
> left to silence..."

Many of these situations in which people feel alone or isolated have a pastoral connotation.

But they are also, fundamentally, diaconal issues, when church members, comfortable in their own values, norms and way of life, resist observing people who are different, and fail to seek to be aware of the hidden needs and longings of others in the congregation. Naturally we cannot ever really know everything of other people. But we can be more open to others, more concerned with observing their visible needs, and more careful in our public words and deeds.

Suffering and need do not occur only among marginalized members of society, for loneliness – and other kinds of lack – are common phenomena. So we see – again – that diakonia has to do with how church members relate to one another as people in need, a need that is sometimes unbearable. The pervasiveness of loneliness as part of our societal life is something we can recognize in the work of an artist I will introduce in an intermezzo.

Immense desolation covered by the zest for living: the works of Sam Taylor-Wood

Many old churches have an altarpiece, either in one piece or consisting of several volets, and beneath this main scene a kind of painted plinth,

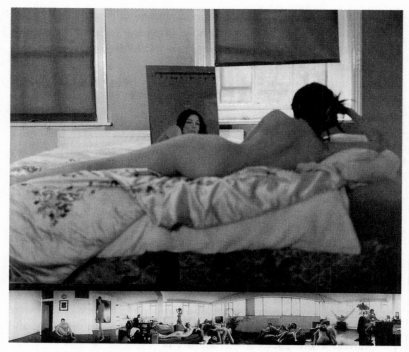

Figure 6.1. Sam Taylor-Wood, Soliloqui III, in: Bulletin Stedelijk Museum
Amsterdam, 1/2002, p. 5

called a predella. Since predelle are by their nature horizontal, long and
narrow, they are often narrative paintings, sometimes making use of continuous representation.

Sam Taylor-Wood made use of this arrangement in three works, called
Soliloqui I, II, III. Each work comprising two parts: a large staged portrait, 180 x 250 cm, and beneath it a smaller panoramic photograph, a
continuous representation. The portrait of *Soliloqui III* (figure 6.1)
depicts a beautiful female nude lying self-assuredly on a bed. With her
back to the camera, we see her face in a mirror which has been positioned

behind the bed. The expression of the woman looking at and examining herself is self-confident, cool, proud. The image is a reference to Velazquez' *Venus with the mirror* from 1650. In the frieze under the portrait we see a group of people, a few of whom are unashamedly – yet also impassively – engaging in sexual activity. Men and women wander naked through the room and in the middle of the virtually empty white interior a couple copulate.

In all of the three works the person in the large photograph recurs in the predella. The woman on the bed reappears in the panoramic scene, wearing a red dress, sitting apart from the activity in an armchair, her eyes closed. The word "Soliloqui" is a term used in the theatre. It is a theatrical device in which an actor steps out of his role for a moment and directly addresses the audience. In Taylor-Wood's *Soliloqui* this device is visualized by the individual pose of the main figure. In *Soliloqui III* the beautiful, serene woman is musing. Where about? The scene in the predella is far from serene, and depicts the atmosphere of ultimate experience in our "experience society". She is present, but apart, dressed in red, her eyes closed, or perhaps, she is only there in her thoughts. "The panoramic scene acts as a mental space, a space where the thoughts and desires of the person portrayed are played out. ...Outward appearance and inner reality are clearly divided."[2]

"With this composition of altarpiece and predella Taylor-Wood tries to lump together the tangible and the intangible, the conscious and the subconscious."[3]

Soliloqui I and II follow the same scheme. The large portrait depicts a person in a characteristic pose, while his or her inner longings are depicted in the predella. The figures obviously long for some special experience with others, contacts which seem to be promising. But it also looks as though they are already anticipating the fiasco: in the lower scene they sit like outsiders, and everything that the others do with one another is in no way communal, but is instead an entirely egocentric exhibition.

Taylor-Wood's work is beautiful and at the same time it creates a sense of sadness. At 34, the artist had already survived two kinds of cancer. Her works radiate a tragic form of optimism. Other photographs and films by Taylor-Wood also show lonely people who have got something into their heads, and will surely experience exciting things, but each of them is busy only with her or his own affairs and does not have any contact with other people, even though this seems to be their deepest longing.

Taylor-Wood's self-portraits reveal the same feelings of "immense loneliness. It is her strength to present this loneliness in a form that is as tense as it is clear".

The work of Taylor-Wood is a telling account of Schulze's idea of the experience society, and of loneliness that is not relieved by experience.

The project "Solitude and diaconal awareness"

The second group of students worked with the same issue of solitude, but went in a completely different direction. They observed people in the street who surely must feel in some way set apart and lonely, owing to a physical handicap like being blind or using a wheelchair. How can we gain knowledge of the experience and feelings of these people? The solution of the group was to divide the other students into two groups, and to assign one person of each group to spend a few hours in a wheelchair, unaware that three others were watching her or him.

One of the "wheelchair-bound" students was given the task of getting copies made at a copy shop. The other students hid near the shop to observe. The student in the wheelchair, an athlete in his thirties, approached the shop quickly, but at the door he had to stop, as the door had a threshold that was far too high to be entered by a person in a wheelchair. As the man waited outside the door, a customer went in, glanced quickly at him, but said nothing. In describing the experience later, the student who had played the part of the man in wheelchair said, "I didn't blame her. When I sat down in the wheelchair my first thought was, OK, here you are, now you have to take care of yourself." The woman hesitated and he asked if she could help him get into the shop, which she did.

The student in the wheelchair made his way to the first copier, but the top was too high for him to reach. He said, "I felt awkward. The owner did not offer to help. I went over to him and he had to make the copies for me, which was very embarrassing." After the student had paid and the owner had helped him back out onto the street, the rest of the group came out of their hiding-places.

The second group stationed themselves near a post office. The "victim" was given the task of buying some stamps at the post office, which could only be entered by climbing six steps. However, the student in the wheelchair, a gray-haired woman, could not even get near the post office because the sidewalk was full of bicycles, mopeds and even a motorcycle. Passers-by were forced to step off the street and walk between parked and moving cars, just to get by. The woman in the wheelchair did the same, going back to the corner where she could leave the sidewalk. At last she stood just across from the stairs leading up to the post office, but still on the street (figure 6.2). She looked

Figure 6.2. Wheelchair user at the post office

around helplessly, for she had no way of getting up the curb and up the steps to the post office. A number of people passed her without stopping. The group watching from their hiding place was worried about their companion on the street in the wheelchair, though she looked unconcerned. After some time a man stopped to ask if she needed help. He helped her onto the sidewalk and went into the post office to buy the stamps, but soon came back empty-handed. As the student later related, the man had entered the post office and found a long line-up at the counter. He was in a hurry, so he came back and excused himself, but told the woman that there was a bookshop that sold stamps less than a hundred yards from the corner. He helped the woman in the wheelchair back onto the street, past all the bicycles, back onto the sidewalk, and pointed the way to the shop. Then he went about his business. The woman said afterward that she was "astonished" by his helpfulness.

This experience made us aware that the physically handicapped are often invisible. If we do perceive them, we may be alert and willing to help, but often we are too busy with our own affairs. The group also discovered many practical problems. Thanks to government projects and policies, the Netherlands, like most Western countries, have made many improvements designed to assist blind people and wheelchair users. Traffic lights have acoustic signals and at many intersections the curbs are sloped to be safe for wheelchairs. These measures may lead us to believe that we live in a country where everything is accessible to the physically disabled but, as these few observations demonstrate, there are many obstacles to people with handicaps. An able-bodied person may be annoyed at having to step onto the street to get around bicycles, delivery trucks, carelessly parked cars or construction barricades. For people in wheelchairs or with other physical handicaps, however, these are impassable obstacles. Not only are they restricted by their disability, but they are further set apart, again and again, by barriers of all kinds, including ignorance, carelessness and apathy.

The project "Drop-in center"

The members of the third group chose drop-in centers as their topic. They visited two such centers in order to gain direct experience of the centers, their clients and the people who work there. At one of the centers, in Leeuwarden, the visitors were quarreling, and the row ended in a free-for-all. One of the students described her experience thus: "I felt very uneasy and left the center without talking to any of the visitors. Once I got back home, I realized that I had simply been afraid in that bizarre setting." The atmosphere at the second center, in Groningen, seemed much more normal. There, she said, " I had a good talk with two visitors and felt all right. I was impressed by the life story of one of them; I hope he is able to stay off drugs and the misery of being addicted."

> *Gone*
> What has happened is gone
> Never I will experience this again
> I hope God strengthens me.
> I don't want to look back
> standing still makes no sense
> I devote myself to the future.

The three students talked with the leaders of the two centers about their work with people suffering from mental illness or addiction. "Meeting them made me feel how lucky I am to have my home and my family. But I cannot get their problems out of my head. The volunteers who work at the center feel the same way."

Most of the people who come to the drop-in center are homeless and the rest live very lonely lives. Many use hard drugs. In the relatively small town of Groningen, with a population of 180,000, there are more than a thousand addicts, the highest ratio in the Netherlands.

Figure 6.3. Collage of an open house

Dream
I often dream of an over-dose
I often dream of the death
and the calm I then will have
though this may sound idiotic.
I often dream that my soul
has stayed on earth after life.
I often dream of earth's future
of lives of people without value.
I often dream that I am falling
from a high mountain into a deep ravine
then I awake in a sweat
and think with some regret
that it was just a dream.

The group made a large collage, 3 meters by 1 meter, resembling the work Drawing the Line by the Canadian art collective that was discussed in section 2.5. There were photographs, cartoons, texts and poems – like the ones above – by people suffering from addiction and social estrangement. The group had to abandon the idea of a "comment wall" because the projects were not shown in a long-term exhibition. Instead of they played music that reflected the theme, and asked us to look at the pictures and texts and discuss them afterwards (figure 6.3).

If only...
If only I had listened
to all that good advice
whispered to me.
If things had gone differently
perhaps I would have seen it earlier.
In a world full of people, so different,
my choice of how to live is simply not accepted.
Solitude, sorrow, cold, hunger, anger and
thoughts all beginning with
if only...
A step in the right direction can bring
happiness, health and relief.
Yet it's my own hell I stay in,
I am in a fix, don't see a way.
Giving all good responses,
but drowning myself in despondency.
No help for me is near
If only... then I would not sit here.

Evaluation

The students appreciated the course very much. It was a new learning experience for them. Though only part of them filled out the questionaire, I can, with the help of my own observations, draw some conclusions.

The first group was already certain about the existence of the problem of loneliness in the congregation. But through their work in the group and the process of making the video, they learned more about the topic. Perhaps the most interesting thing to them was developing a means of showing the congregation the problem in a simple and immediate way.

They even indicated how to manage the problem. Loneliness can not be eliminated, but it can be seen and understood in some way. That in itself will help.

One of the group members wrote: "Our discussions and exchange of ideas were very inspiring. While producing the video, we were constantly changing the music, the poems, the pictures, and this deepened our insight in the problem of loneliness in the congregation. We found that we had to really understand the problem in order to find ways to perform it in a realistic and meaningful way. Even if we had never shown our performance on video, the process of working together intensified our consciousness with regard to diakonia."

The second group made it very easy for us to understand their thoughts and feelings, because they invited us to participate directly in their experiments. One of them wrote that he could foresee his feelings about the outcome of the wheelchair experiments. He expected to feel more concern for students in the wheelchairs because he knew them so well. "When you see a stranger, an unknown person", he observed, "you feel much less involved." His honest statement affirms what I have said in Chapter 3, namely, as Jesus said in the Sermon on the Mount, that by nature we want to take care of ourselves and those close to us. To realize diakonia, however, we need to go beyond.

In practical terms, the group became aware of the variety of possible ways of helping or not helping. Most people ignore people with a handicap; some are too quick in offering help. The best way to offer help, the group found, is to be aware of fellow human beings with an handicap but to wait until you are sure that help is wanted before offering it. Almost as terrible as being neglected is to feel oneself to be prey for another person's desire to be helpful.

The third group, which opted for direct experience, made clear by their performance that the experience had affected them deeply. The student who was upset by the fighting at one of the drop-in centers nevertheless had an unforgettable experience that made her strongly aware of the huge problems of drug addicts and of the people who work with them.

Another member of this group used the diaconal theory that is outlined here in Chapters 3 and 4, to understand her experiences at the drop-in center. She wrote down her thoughts and conclusions: "Being near to people, trying to make connections with the regular visitors, trying to let them experience something of the celebrations. This also means taking people seriously, seeing them as equals, so not always agreeing with or affirming their life stories, which are tragic, but also talking to them as responsible people. People often have lived through terrible things, but ultimately they themselves are responsible for their addiction."

This group once again showed how working together on a performance or installation about a subject in the sphere of ethics and human values, in this case an issue concerning the ministry of mercy and justice, helps to promote the transformation of one's frame of reference. The process of grappling intensely with the thoughts and feelings of other people about situations of need and suffering, and experiencing the issue together from various points of view can transform the way we think about it. This is what Ricoeur would call a 'transfiguration': leaving behind old beliefs and behaviours and embracing a new and better comprehension[4].

6.3. Becoming Part of the Scene: Longing for a Safe Home for all Human Beings...

My objective of enabling the students to better empathize with people in situations of unbearable need was not realized with all students. Forty hours was not enough time for everybody to change their beliefs and behaviours, but everyone learned a great deal about teaching in the congregation.

These performances were not works of art; I did not expect or hope that they would be. The purpose of these exercises in consciousness-raising, as I have pointed out in Chapter 2, is not to produce artists or artworks but to expand the awareness of members of the congregation by helping them to learn to observe humanity and the world in accordance with the vision of the Jewish prophets, of Jesus, and of heroes of the faith such as Francis of Assisi, Dietrich Bonhoeffer and Martin Luther King. Their vision of a better world, of justice and mercy for all creatures, of the Kingdom of God here and now, determined their way of observing and acting in the world. God's own longing for goodness and for the end of all kinds of suffering, became their own longing.

One of the students expressed this very simply when she wrote:

> "Sometimes I feel awfully cold. I cannot bear it and must look for a warm shelter. Happily, I can go to my own safe and welcoming home. When I saw those people at night, in winter, living on the street, I felt a terrible cold. How I long for a safe home for all human beings..."

This utterance was part of their performance. Our deepest longings for enjoyment and relief of every kind of unbearable need can be intensified by making performances and installations. Excellent examples abound in postmodern art. The artists and works that I have presented in this book, and many others, are examples of the willingness to see and react to the injustice and wrongs that exist all around, for those who dare to observe.

Here I present one last example, a work by Janet Cardiff, who invites the visitor to experience her work from within her own mind. Once you agree to enter you will never escape...

The walk

Cardiff has designed several walks[5] like the one in Münster (figure 6.4 and 4b) and the one installed at the PS1. Museum of Contemporary Art, winter 2001/2002. Each walk is accompanied by a map and a CD; visitors are provided with a map and a headset to guide them along the way. I accepted the PS1 offer and walked through parts of the strange building, once a school. The woman's voice in my ears entered into me like the seductive voices of the sirens calling to the rowers, their ears stuffed up, when Ulysses, tied to the mast, made his way past their treacherous rocks. But Cardiff's voice is far from treacherous. I had the agreeable feeling of being the owner of that voice, of living in a woman's body, of tripping up stairs on dainty shoes, gasping a little when going

Figure 6.4. Janet Cardiff's walk in Münster, in: C. Christov-Bakargiev, *Janet Cardiff. A Survey of Works Including Collaborations with George Bures Miller*, PS1.MoMA, Long Island City 2001, p. 86f

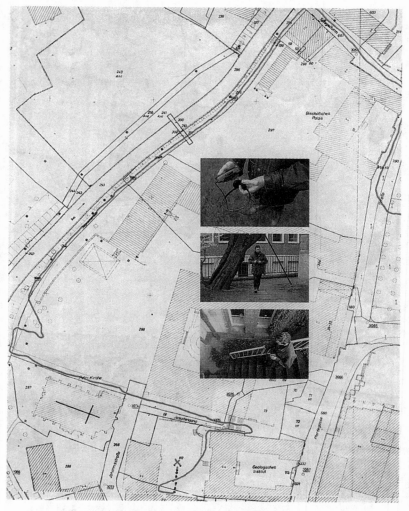

Figure 6.4b. Janet Cardiff's walk in Münster, in: C. Christov-Bakargiev, *Janet Cardiff. A Survey of Works Including Collaborations with George Bures Miller*, PS1.MoMA, Long Island City 2001, p. 86f

up and walking across the slightly squeaking parquet floor. It was curious to me that I never lost my way during the fourteen minutes I followed the voice, despite all twists and turns, never knowing exactly where I was, in long, narrow gangways, on stairs, in a large hall, on a chair. Sometimes in semi-darkness – "be careful", but also, "don't be afraid" and "feel how quiet this place is…" And then at the end "now I must go, you will find your way, bye bye…"

Cardiff's walk is the last of my suggestions that can be adapted for the purpose of making one's own performance. There are many possibilities to fill such a walk with meaningful contents, in our case on a subject related to diakonia, the ministry of mercy and justice. Cardiff herself does not explicitly address social issues in her works, but they can readily be adapted to a variety of themes, including social and diaconal ones. What her work does, above all, is to make the viewer or participant the center of the 'play'. When the structure is in place, thoughts and emotions will come up of themselves to fill it.

As one of the students in the "k.o.9" study group wrote: "How I long for a safe home for all human beings…"

Our deepest longings for enjoyment and for relief of every kind of unbearable lack can be intensified by making performances and installations. Being yourself in the midst of the performance, your thoughts and physical feelings cannot miss the 'play'. Do we dare to become part of the scene? Many artists dare to observe…

Do we?

NOTES
(Numbers per chapter)

Prologue

[1] A.K. Ploeger, J.J. Ploeger-Grotegoed, *De gemeente en haar verlangen. Van praktische theologie naar de geloofspraktijk van de gemeenteleden* ("The Congregation and its Longing. From Practical Theology to the Practice of the Church Members"), Kampen 2001. I will refer to this study as "Handbook PT".

[2] R. Inglehart, *Culture Shift in Advanced Industrial Society*, Princeton 1990, p. 187.

[3] G. Schulze, *Die Erlebnisgesellschaft*, Frankfurt 1992 (translated in English as *The Experience Society*). See also the beginning of Chapter 1.

[4] This thesis is worked out at length in our Handbook PT.

[5] I will seldom speak about the history of art and art historians. My concern is the philosophical meaning of postmodern art, so I draw on the work of philosophers of art like Dickie, Danto, Cauquelin, Seel, Welsch; cf. the title of a study by A.A. van den Braembussche (Bussum 1996): *Denken over kunst* (Thinking about art). In any case *traditional* art historians have little useful insight to offer into postmodern art, cf. H. Miedema, *Kunst historisch*, Leiden 1995. Of course, as postmodern art becomes more accepted, *contemporary* art historians, like Hans Belting, are also becoming more involved in this aspect of art criticism. But the difference is clear, see H. Belting et al., *Kunstgeschichte. Eine Einführung*, Berlin 1996, pp. 149f.

[6] With thanks to Dr. Lisa Hess (Princeton) for her remark on this point. Cf. E.A. McKee, *Diakonia in the Classical Reformed Tradition and Today*, p. 4. Another good entrance to the problem is the opposition, discussed below, of aisthesis and anaisthesis (Welsch).

Chapter 1.

[1] Quotations from G. Schulze, *Erlebnisgesellschaft*, note pro-3, pp. 37; 427ff; 455. In his research on the experience society, Schulze found an empirical basis for his hypotheses that people who were under the age of forty (in the 1980s) enjoy the combination of bodily reactions and cognitive representations. "Our (western) Experience Society is to be understood, in comparison

with other historical and cultural societies, as an inner-oriented constructed social world" (i.e. "everyday-aesthetical", directed to the beautiful) (p. 39, 732, 735). Cf. pp. 77, 105f, 254, 363, 738. "The relation between consciousness and body is reciprocal. (...) First consciousness conditions the body in conformity with certain schemes, and afterwards consciousness acts in conformity with the body. Consciousness develops forms of movement and blockades of movement, attitudes, physiological routines, fitting in schemes of enjoyment like contemplation, sociability and action" (363; depending on the "milieu").

2   G. Schulze, *Kulissen des Glücks. Streifzüge durch die Eventkultur*, Campus, Frankfurt/New York 1999/2000. Quotations from p. 7, 10, 11 and 102.

3   What does Schulze mean by the term "beautiful life" ("das schöne Leben"? The use of this phrase goes back to Greek philosophy. Aristotle sometimes combined "the beautiful and the good" in one word when he spoke of "kalokagathy" (J. Hirschberger, *Geschichte der Philosophie*, Bd. I, Freiburg 1976/1991, p. 231). For Kant there was a gap between the good and the aesthetic, and the aesthetic he divides again into the pleasant ("Angenehmen"), the beautiful ("Schöne") and the sublime ("Erhabene"; I. Kant, *Kritik der Urteilskraft*, 1790, Ed. Weischedel, Frankfurt 1995, pp. 191ff.). Concerning the difference between goodness and beauty Kant gives "a metaphysical interpretation of aesthetic experience: it makes us conscious of a connection that we have with the world, and with one another, which lies beyond the empirical world. Beauty therefore has a semi-religious and moral significance for Kant. Kant calls beauty the 'symbol of the good'" (S. Gardner, "Aesthetics", in: N. Bunnin et al. (eds.), *The Blackwell Companion to Philosophy*, Oxford 1996, p. 233). It seems to me that Schulze gives the "beautiful life" the same meaning as Aristotle, but he uses it top-down, no longer meaning evident fronèsis, practical reason, from the outer world and the ethical good and beautiful way of life, but rather an inner feeling of "It pleases me" (Schulze, note 1.1, p. 39). Here, Aristotle, in his *Ethica Nicomachea*, is more stringent and distinguishes pleasure which is directed to the highest, the perfect good, from pleasure which is not.

4   "However, the social construction of reality takes place somewhere else – in discussions ("Diskursen") between economics, technology, science, politics and the public sphere." (But) "events are no more the place for the necessarily continued discussion, while discussions are no events. The first of these two statements has already culturally occurred, whereas we still have to work on the second" (103). Compare U. Volkmann, "Das Projekt des schönen Lebens – Gerhard Schulzes "Erlebnisgesellschaft", in U. Schimank (ed.), *Soziologische Gegenwartsdiagnosen I*, UTB 2158, 2000, pp. 86-88.

5   Schulze, Kulissen, p. 82, 87.

[6] W. Welsch, *Vernunft. Die zeitgenössische Vernunftkritik und das Konzept der transversalen Vernunft*, STW 1238, Frankfurt/M 1996. This possibility of links between the subjective event-world and the social world, including politics and economy, is a subject I addressed in A.K. Ploeger, *Diskurs*, 's Gravenhage 1989. Here, I only recall the ideas about intermediary groups between private and public spheres put forward by the Dutch sociologist Zijdervelt, the French Wieviorka and the Spanish Castells, see our Handbook PT, pp. 421ff and 442ff. In the present study, *Dare We Observe?*, I try to make clear how we can use our (post-)modern way of experiencing *through events* such as art performances, to develop our skills of observing the *social world* as a world full of distress.

[7] My approach to the relationship between religion and art differs from the familiar approaches like the description or re-use of religious and sacred art or even the use of secular art to illustrate Christian insights. Close to my ideas about religion and art are the insights of the American theologian Frank Burch Brown, especially in his studies *Religious Aesthetics. A Theological Study of Making and Meaning*, Princeton 1989, and *Good Taste, Bad Taste and Christian Taste. Aesthetics in Religious Life*, Oxford 2000. Our views on the interrelatedness – and differences – between religion and art do not differ significantly. But our respective intentions are different.

[8] Parts of this chapter where published in A.K. Ploeger, "The Common Sources of Art and Religion: Some Proposals on the Aesthetic Side of Practical Theology", in: P. Ballard (ed.), *Creativity, Imagination and Criticism. The Expressive Dimensions in Practical Theology*, Cardiff 2001.

[9] The distinction between this subjective event-world and the social world, characterized as "the risk society" or "reflective modernization", is maintained; see U. Beck, *Risikogesellschaft*, Frankfurt/M 1987; U. Beck, A. Giddens, S. Lash, *Reflexive Modernisierung*, Frankfurt 1996; J. de Mul, *De informatisering van het wereldbeeld*, in: Dies Natalis Erasmus Universiteit Rotterdam 1997, pp. 9-26; R. Münch, *Globale Dynamik, lokale Lebenswelten. Der schwierige Weg in die Weltgesellschaft*, STW 1342, Frankfurt/M 1998. Walter Benjamin used the term in a very negative judgment about the fascist art-manifesto of the futuristic painter Marinetti, who wrote in 1936, during Mussolini's Ethiopian War, about the "Aestheticization of the War": "War is beautiful.... creating well designed tanks, geometric flying squadrons and smoke spirals of burning villages... true aesthetics of war..." (W. Benjamin, "The Work of Art in the Era of its Technical Reproducibility", in idem, *Gesammelte Schriften Bd I-2*, STW 931, pp. 506f. See also R. Bubner, *Aesthetische Erfahrung*, NF 564, Frankfurt/M. 1989, pp. 149ff (negative); Baudrillard, *La transparence du mal*, Galilée, Paris 1997.

[10] Walter Pichler, *Drawings: Sculptures: Buildings*, Stedelijk Museum Amsterdam 1998; ISBN 3851270193.

[11] In Chapter 2 I will call original aesthetic and religious experiences – with some restrictions – pure *spiritual* experiences. See A.K. Ploeger, "The Importance of Spirituality for Intercultural Learning", in: Albert Ploeger & Carl Sterkens (eds.), *Search for Meaning. Education into Realms of Meaning in a Plural Society,* Kampen 1998, pp. 129-162. Spirituality is one of the possibilities of transversal reason (Welsch), bridging different perspectives, like theories and feelings in religion and art.

[12] H.R. Armstrong, *The Transmission of Faith Through Art,* in: Communio, Summer 2001, pp. 386-397. The title of Armstrong's article already frankly suggests that art might bring people back to the church. He quotes the sociologist Wuthnow as saying that "many Americans are now turning to artists for spiritual guidance"; these artists "speak more comfortably about sprituality than about organized religion". "Spirits are as much uplifted by the concert on Saturday as by the sermon on Sunday morning." Armstrong suggests that the art of many artists who are not Christians is spiritually devilish (394), so Christians should make their own art. This antithetical vision is neither shared by many organizers of exhibitions on art and religion nor by most authors who write about the use of art in Christian preaching and learning. See for example R. Steensma e.a., *Jezus is boos. Het beeld van Christus in de hedendaagse kunst,* Zoetermeer 1995; J. de Wal, *Kunst zonder kerk,* Utrecht 1999; R. Quaghebeur, D. Verbiest (ed.), *Epifanie. Actuele kunst en religie,* Leuven 2000; M. Barnard, *Wat het oog heeft gezien. Verbeelding als sleutel van het credo,* Zoetermeer 1997; P. Sherry, *Spirit and Beauty: An Introduction to Theological Aesthetics,* Oxford 1992; J.N. Corbitt, *The Sound of the Harvest: Music in Global Christianity,* Grand Rapids 1998; J.B. Begbie, *Beholding the Glory. Incarnation through the Arts,* Grand Rapids 2000; J.W. de Cruchy, *Christianity, Art and Transformation. Theological Aesthetics in the Struggle for Justice,* Cambridge 2001. Particularly outstanding examples are the works of F.B. Brown, mentioned in note 1.7, and A. Grözinger, *Praktische Theologie und Aesthetik,* Kaiser 1987; idem, *Praktische Theologie als Kunst der Wahrnehmung,* Gütersloh 1995.
A famous essay on art from a more general spiritual standpoint is W. Kandinsky's *Concerning the Spiritual in Art,* New York 1947 (originally published in German as: *Ueber das Geistige in der Kunst,* München 1912; Dutch: *Spiritualiteit en abstractie in de kunst,* Zeist 1987). See also R. Lipsey, *An Art of Our Own. The Spiritual in Twentieth Century Art,* Boston & London 1997.

[13] This can also be true for other areas of culture and nature. Here, however, I am only comparing religion and art, and art can be any type of art, though I speak especially about visual art. Moreover I do not consider the many other theories about religious experiences. Our approach uses ideas from different perspectives, such as the opposing philosophers of art Wolfgang Welsch, *Undoing*

Aesthetics, London, etc. 1997 and Martin Seel, *Die Kunst der Entzweiung*, Suhrkamp, Frankfurt/M 1985; idem, *Ethisch-ästhetische Studien*, STW 1249, Frankfurt 1996. Welsch sees a continuum between 'formal' art and 'aisthesis', observation of everyday life; Seel wants to set aside a separate space for aesthetics, as "vollzugsorientiert" (goal-oriented) and "selbstbezüglich" (self-referential)(i.e. the goal is observation in itself; Seel 1996, 48f).
R. Bubner, in *Aesthetische Erfahrung*, note 1.9, pp. 38, 127, 139f., like Kant, does not want to fixate aesthetic experience, and consequently does not even complete what we call below phase 1 of the process of experiencing. The second component, incorporation in one's own frame of reference, is lacking. Perhaps it is better to use the phrase that Jüngel, as well as Bubner and Seel, borrowed from Heidegger, and which Jüngel applied to religious experiences and Bubner (p. 118) and Seel to aesthetic ones: to have an experience with experience (with things in everyday life). To see God in a burning bush; to see something world-transforming in a Brillo box. See further on the discussion of the transfiguration of the commonplace.

[14] I owe this theory of phases to P. Ricoeur, *From Text to Action*, Evanston 1991 (texts in French from 1975-1986), though I use it in my own way. Another French writer, Anne Cauquelin, *Petit traité d'art contemporain*, Paris 1996, also has an interesting view on phases in the observing and understanding of artworks; see note 1.36.

[15] P. Tillich, "Contemporary Visual Arts and the Revelatory Character of Style", in: idem, *On Art and Architecture*, New York 1987, p. 130.

[16] Part of the exhibition *Surface*, at the Institute of Contemporary Art, Philadelphia, January 2002.

[17] Welsch describes the complementariness of aesthetic and anaesthetic behaviour. Anaesthesis can be physical blunting as well as spiritual blindness. It is also the 'cool state' at the end of everyday processes of aestheticization like entertainment and watching television. It has to do with living in an era of information that produces 'new inconveniences' we have to cope with, often not really wanting to see the complexity and the paradoxes that bring disappointment and new uncertainty. See W. Welsch, "Aesthetik und Anaesthetik", in: Welsch, *Aesthetisches Denken*, Reclam, Stuttgart 1990, pp. 9-40; 63-68; 72, 206; J. Habermas, *Die neue Unübersichtlichkeit*, Frankfurt 1985; compare Schulze, Erlebnisgesellschaft, pp. 36; 60-67.

[18] For instance, in a reproduction of Michelangelo's frescos in the Sistine Chapel in Rome, Grifalconi replaced God the father and Christ with females figures.

[19] G. Dickie, *Introduction to Aesthetics. An Analytical Approach*, New York, Oxford 1997, p. 15.

[20] M. Archer, *Art Since 1960*, London 1997, p. 215.

[21] A.C. Danto, *The Transfiguration of the Commonplace*, Harvard, Cambridge (M), 1981. The American Danto and the German historian of art Hans Belting, perhaps the best known art critics in their respective countries, wrote almost at the same moment about the end of art. But later on they corrected themselves and referred instead to the end of art history. H. Belting, *Das Ende der Kunstgeschichte*, Beck, München 1995; A.C. Danto, "Narratives of the End of Art", in: *Encounter and Reflections*, New York 1986, pp. 331ff.

[22] A.C. Danto, *After the End of Art. Contemporary art and the pale of history*, Princeton Un. Press, Princeton 1997 (The Mellon Lectures in Fine Art, Washington). Since then Danto has qualified his views once again, in *The Madonna of the Future*, Berkeley 2000/2001. Danto calls himself an essentialist and a historian. As an essentialist, he wants to define art in terms of sufficient and necessary conditions. 'Essence' has two meanings that must not be confounded: first, referring to a class of things, marked by a term (denotative or extensional), and second, referring to a set of attributes that connote with the term (connotative or intensional). Working in an extensional way happens by induction, when we strive to unearth the attributes which are normal and specific for the items that form the extension of a term. "The extension of a concept (or a term) will be all and only those things that fall under the concept – the robins and sparrows and ducks if the concept is 'bird'. (...) The intension comprises all the conditions deemed necessary for something to be classed as a bird – wingedness, oviparousness, and the like" (1997, p. 425). It seems to be no more possible to group the multiple forms of postmodern art – extensional – in the same class as art from Giotto unto Pollock; if we see art as "artwork", we can only question its "family resemblance", that is, its intensionality. I am not sure whether Danto's definition stands up to close scrutiny.

[23] Elsewhere Danto writes that there are critics who maintain: "The primary question for me about works of art is what they are rather than what they mean. One of the things that is wrong with a lot of art that is highly praised is that it can only be experienced in its 'meaning' because what it is is so negligible that you're being invited to respond to its posted agenda, not what the artist has actually made for you to look at." In Danto's vision, however, "the being of a work of art *is* its meaning" (2000, note 1.22, p. x).

[24] "The concept of art, as essentialist, is timeless. But the extension of the term is historically indexed" (1997, note 1.22, p. 196).

[25] Danto, 2000, note 1.22, p. xi.

[26] Danto 2000, note 1.22, p. 430; my emphasis.

[27] These means can be anything, for "the art supply store would have to be as rich as the inventory of life" (2000, note 1.22, p. 430).

[28] Danto 1997, note 1.22, p. 216.

[29] ... "and Warhol, who had won prize after prize as one of New York's leading commercial artists, would have been the first to appreciate its value"; Danto, 2000, note 1.22, p. XXV.

[30] Appropriationist artists, like Levine and Bidlo, grabbed work from earlier times in order to critique, and by doing so used it to provide their own income... (as Warhol did, though in another sense, with Harvey's work).

[31] "It is to imagine what could be meant by the object if it were the vehicle of an artistic statement" (2000, note 1.22, p. XXIX).

[32] According to the famous critic, Margolis (J. Margolis, *Farewell to Danto and Goodman*, in: British Journal of Aesthetics, 38/4, October 1998, pp. 353-374), both Danto and Goodman miss the point when they speak about "the constructive realism of artworks and about the perceptual standing of the properties of paintings". Both give an unacceptable 'reductio'. "They fail sans phrase". Margolis' solution is to say that "works of art are physically embodied but cultural appearing (real) things. To him works of art do not need a philosophical "artistic identification" (Danto's 'ascribed meaning').
I choose a position between Danto and Margolis. On the one hand, with Seel, I consider a work of art everything that a forum of distinguished art critics calls "gelungen", "being successful" (Seel, *Entzweiung*, note 1.13, p. 228, 305). On the other hand, an artwork that is 'not successful' according to 'distinguished art critics', can be so enlightening, e.g. because of its ethical meaning, that I consider it real art by a "coup de joueur" (a trick of the player of a game), as Cauquelin, note 1.14, calls it. She suggests that contemporary art goes back from traditional artworks to the thing (la chose); "it works against the finished ideas" of earlier - premodern or modern (A.P.) – art". She speaks of the world of art as "le jeu", the game (25), and about the rules of this game (28). The contemporary site of art is textual (32ff), and this connects her views to those of Dickie and Danto. However, she rejects Danto's earlier theory of the Brillo box. To her the "real" and the Warhol Brillo box are both "objets à notice" (objects with explicit or implicit instructions for use, as a chair or a CD player); we can only call it an object of art when we take away the traditional idea of the 'doxa' of an artwork, "en les imposant commes esthétiques, par une décision, un 'coup' de joueur" (57). Cauquelin broadens the meaning of doxa, and suggests approaches to criticism (see note 1.36).

[33] Danto, 1997, note 1.22, p. 129. Further on I will relate similar thoughts that I had as a theologian.

[34] Danto 1997, note 1.22, p. 89.

[35] Welsch developed his idea about understanding Reason as transversality in W. Welsch, *Unsere postmoderne Moderne*, Weinheim 1988, pp. 295ff. He compares types of rationality such as economic, ethical and aesthetical reasoning.

They have their own domains, but these domains overlap. Art seen as "l'art pour l'art" differs from art seen as "art and life", "The first type leads to the temple of muses, the latter to freed existence" (298). There are conflicting "questions of conpossibility" as Welsch calls them, between the domains of 'economics' and 'art and life' (299ff). Conflicts also mean overlaps, and this is part of transversal reason. See also Welsch, *Denken*, note 1.17, p. 72, 206; idem, *Vernunft*, note 1.6, passim; here, especially p. 369 and p. 762; idem, "AESTHET/HICS", in: *Undoing*, note 1.13, p. 60-77 (also in C. Wulf e.a., *Ethik und Aesthetik*, Berlin 1994, p. 3-22.

36 Welsch discerns four steps: simple observation, conjecture of 'sense' (together phase 1); reflection and testing (phase 2); and total view of the area of the phenomenon, often leading to critical ethical remarks. W. Welsch, *Denken*, note 1.17, p. 49. The phases presented here also correspond to the phases of a practical-theologian research project, see our Handbook PT. Cauquelin, *Petit traité*, note 1.14, 47ff., speaks of the *doxa* of an artwork, a kind of aesthetic logic, which has to do with the "humeurs, pressions environnantes (le milieu) et dispositions à croire", the temper, context and disposition of the viewers of a work to believe certain things – or not. Following Kant, Cauquelin decribes four moments of the aesthetic judgement (56ff): The doxa starts with 'disinterestedness' (corresponding to my phase 1a), though always with regard to the viewer's frame of reference (my phase 1b) but also praises education in arts: 'neutralization' (my phase 2). Moreover the doxa wants a work of art to be 'unique', original, or – as in the case of Brillo boxes – present a new intention (also part of my phase 2). The fourth moment Cauquelin mentions is "communiquer", which has to do with all of the preceding moments, and thus corresponds to my phase 3. Moral or discursive activities are part of the "coups d'artistes avant-garde", to open discourse. A work of art must not be informative, but rather educational ("il doit nous enseigner et non nous renseigner"). Everybody must have the chance to share, and to win by sharing. Therefore, as Umberto Eco says, we need open works of art: each artist respecting the limits of – succesful – interpretation of her or his work, but also leaving opportunities for viewers to make new discoveries, depending on their lifeworld. See Cauquelin, op.cit., pp. 47ff. on doxa and pp. 56ff. on the moments of judgement.

37 Cauquelin, *Petit traité*, note 1.14, p. 110 (we no longer talk about figuration but about "trans-figuration"), and p. 176 (some think of art as a new religion, but to me it is always a game, though working on art is always working in the spirit of "ultimate painting", p. 178).

38 H. Schwebel, "Kunst und Religion zwischen Moderne und Postmoderne. Die Situation – Ein neu erwachtes Kunstinteresse" (Art and Religion between Modernity and Postmodernity. The Situation – A Newly Awakened Interest in Art), in: *Kunst und Religion*, Jahrbuch der Religionspädagogik (JRP 13),

Neukirchen 1997, pp. 65ff. P. Tillich, "Art and Ultimate reality", in: idem, *On Art and Architecture*, pp. 139-157. Tillich mentions five "stylistic elements", correlated with "types of religious experience" in artworks, i.e. magical or numinous realism correlated with sacramental religious experience, the mystical type (trying to reach ultimate reality without specific mediating means) in religion as well as in painting in a non-objective style, critical realism and the prophetic-protesting type, the idealistic type and religious humanism, and, last, the expressionistic type, correlated with the ecstatic-spiritual religious type. "The main point in the discussion of the five stylistic elements which can become mediators of ultimate reality has been to show that the manifestation of the ultimate in the visual arts is not dependent on the use of works which traditionally are called religious art" (151).

[39] Welsch himself ignores transcendence and religion completely. He speaks of "Zonen des Unfaßlichen"; "das paradoxe ästhetische Gefühl eines Anästhetische", Welsch, Denken, p. 217; 89. In the same line, Martin describes the area of experiences and reflection between the revealed and the hidden God. G.M. Martin, "Gott auf der Bibliodrama-Bühne: Zum Bibelgebrauch in der Postmoderne", in: B. Beuscher et al. (eds.), *Prozesse postmoderner Wahrnehmung. Kunst-Religion-Pädagogik*, Wien 1996, p. 110.

[40] Handbook PT, Chapter 30: "Believing with body and mind"; S. McFague, *The Body of God: an Ecological Theology*, Minneapolis 1993, pp. 14ff.

[41] Dickie, *Introduction*, note 1.19, pp. 159f.

[42] R. Fuchs on W. Pichler (see note 1.10). Rudi Fuchs is the director of the Stedelijk Museum. Pichler only names his works, and stresses that they function best on the grounds of his property in Burgenland, Austria.

[43] The phrase 'economic Trinity' refers to the three 'faces' or manifestations of God's activity – missions – in the world, correlated with the names Father, Son, and Spirit. The phrase 'immanent Trinity', also called the 'essential' Trinity, points to the reciprocal relationships of Father, Son and Spirit, considered apart from God's activity in the world. C.M. LaCugna, *God For Us. The Trinity and Christian Life*, Harper, San Franscisco 1991, p. 211f.

Chapter 2.

[1] Roy A. Rappaport, *Ritual and Religion in the Making of Humanity*, Cambridge 1999, p. 1. Other quotations: p. 109, 451.

[2] See my article, "The Importance of Spirituality", note 1.11. I refer to Paul Ricoeur, *Time and Narrative*, Part I, Chicago 1984, p. 76; who wrote that stories and other images refigure, or even transfigure, the significance of old insights. Cf. Chapter 1.4 of the present book.

³ Paul Ricoeur, *Time and Narrative*, Part III; Chicago 1988, p. 249.

⁴ This issue is discussed in many studies on religion and art. In our Handbook I argue that Christians believe spirituality to be a gift for all humankind.

⁵ I owe the following distinctions to Raymond Holley, *Religious Education and Religious Understanding. An Introduction to the Philosophy of Religious Education*, London 1978, who calls the spiritual non-rational, non-physical and dynamic.

⁶ Carel Blotkamp, "A Dutchman in New York", in: *New Dutch Sculptors. Job Koelewijn*, published by New Sculpture Museum, Rijssen NL 1999, pp. 10-37.

⁷ Rappaport, Ritual, p. 24, and the following section, pp. 32-50.

⁸ They construct the integrated conventional order, which Rappaport calls "logos". This term does not come from the Bible, but from the Greek philosopher Heraclitus, from whom it was taken up by Heidegger. This order designates moral values, the vision of time and eternity, creation, the holy and the holiness of that order, and other matters like occultism, the numinous, the divine and what I refer to as the basic needs that surpass what can be expressed in words (ibid, 27).

⁹ Werner Jetter, *Symbol und Ritual. Anthropologische Elemente im Gottesdienst*, Göttingen 1978/1986; Ronald L. Grimes, *Ritual Criticism*, Columbia 1990; Gerard Lukken, *Rituelen in overvloed*, Baarn 1999.

¹⁰ Rappaport, Ritual, pp. 458; 346ff.

¹¹ Another problem of rituals and performances as a didactical method is the paradox of ritual, as demonstrated by Zadkine's statue *The Destroyed City* in Rotterdam. The American philosopher Susanne Langer, often cited in literature about ritual, is very aware of this paradox. She makes a sharp distinction between what she calls discursive and presentative symbolism. It is the paradox between investigating and discussing empirical reality, and imagining insensible things. S.K. Langer, *Philosophy In a New Key*, Harvard 1941/1980, 11th ed. from the revised 3rd printing in 1957; idem, *Feeling and Form. A Theory of Art developed from "Philosophy In a New Key"*, London 1953. For a critique of Langer's theory of art see A.K. Ploeger, *De plaats en gestalte van het protestantse ritueel in onze cultuur*, in: Praktische theologie, 2001/4, pp. 457-480.

¹² According to Henk M. Vroom, *Religies en de waarheid*, Kampen 1988, with additions from Jürgen Werbick, *Glauben lernen aus Erfahrung. Grundbegriffe einer Didaktik des Glaubens*, München 1989, pp. 174ff and idem, *Vom Wagnis des Christseins. Wie glaubwürdig ist der Glaube?*, München 1995, pp. 204ff and A.K. Ploeger, *Inleiding in de godsdienstpedagogiek* 2001(5), 104f.

¹³ M. Josuttis, "Der Gottesdienst als Ritual", in: F. Wintzer et al. (eds.), *Praktische Theologie*, Neukirchen 1994, pp. 43-57, here p. 55.

¹⁴ C. Crowston, "The Dark Pool", Brochure from 1995, in: C. Christov-Bakargiev, *Janet Cardiff. A Survey of Works Including Collaborations with George*

Bures Miller, PS1.MoMA, Long Island City 2001, p. 54. The following passages by Cardiff are from the same catalogue.

[15] See note 2.11.

[16] Since Peatling, Oser, Fowler and Bucher we will not forget that children do not envision either the empirical or the imagined world as the same way adults do, cf. F. Schweitzer, *Die Religion des Kindes*, Gütersloh 1992, pp. 401-437. We can further their competences in the domain of dreams, symbols and metaphors. But "Growing up too fast too soon", as David Elkind described *The Hurried Child* (Reading, etc. 1988), is the other side of the coin. In any case, my proposals will be beyond the understanding of young children. For them there are many other possibilities, for example picture books about art like the one by Cristina Cappa Legora, *Andy Warhol*, Mazzota 1996 (available in Italian and German, probably also in English).

[17] Christoffer Reed, "Postmodernism and the Art of Identity", in: N. Stangos (ed.), *Concepts of Modern Art*, London 1994, pp. 271-293; here p. 289.

[18] Texts by the curator of this exhibition at the New Museum of Contemporary Art, winter 2001/2002.

[19] Archer, note 1.20, pp. 119f

[20] Cf. J.W. de Cruchy, *Christianity*, note 1.12, p. 79.

Chapter 3.

[1] W.J.T. Mitchell, *Picture Theory*, Chicago & London 1994, pp. 405f.

[2] Cf. for F.B. Brown, note 1.7; In *Christianity*, note 1.12, de Cruchy, a South African, also says that art has to do with enjoyment and justice (79). Art is 'God-given' (241) by the work of the Spirit (124ff, 238). Though art cannot change society, it can help "us both individually and corporately to perceive reality in a new way, and by so doing, it opens up possibilities of transformation. Nothing better expresses the connection between aesthetics and a concern for social transformation than the linking of the liturgy within the sanctuary and the liturgy of daily life that occurs in the public square, as we do justice, love mercy, and walk humbly with each other and with God" (253; cf. 200). J.D. Brown, *Masks of Mystery. Explorations in Christian Faith and the Arts*, Lanham aso 1997, says: "Muses are to artists as the Holy Spirit is to believers and therefore Muse and Spirit might be the same. (...) Both have their origin in great mystery" (118).

[3] From: Dawn Perlmutter, "The Subjugation of the Spiritual in Art", in D. Perlmutter, D. Koppman, *Reclaiming the Spiritual in Art. Contemporary Cross-Cultural Perspectives*, New York 1999, p. 12. For an interesting, but often disputed view on the 'unity of ethics and aesthetics in ritual', see R. Girard, "Die

Einheit von Ethik und Aesthetik im Ritual", in: C. Wulf et al., *Ethik der Aesthetik*, Berlin 1994, pp. 3-22.

⁴ Including a new reading of the famous Duck-Rabbit picture from *Fliegende Blätter* (1892; later used by Wittgenstein and in psychology) and Magritte's *Ceci n'est pas une pipe* (described by Foucault and Deleuze); see his chapter on *Metapictures* in Mitchell, *Picture Theory*, note 3.1, pp. 35-82.

⁵ See Chapter X, *Diakonia*, in our Handbook PT. The following biblical passages are the ones most frequently quoted in European studies about diaconate: Deut. 26:10-12; Lev. 25; Ps. 113; Jesaja 1-6; 61; Amos; Matthew 20:20-28; 25:31-46; Luke 4:18f; 22; John 13 and Phil. 2:1-11. I suggest adding Luke 6:32-35 and 1 John 4:19f.

⁶ Handbook PT, p. 571; M.E. Kohler, *Diakonie*, Neukirchen 1995, pp. 22f.

⁷ W.J. Hollenweger, *Konflikt in Korinth. Memoiren eines alten Mannes*, München 1978; M.A. Meeks, *The First Urban Christians*, Yale 1983; G. Theissen, *Ik moest van Pilatus achter Jezus aan. Verslag van een speurtocht*, Baarn 1988.

⁸ *Hope for a Global Future*. Towards Just and Sustainable Human Development. Approved by the 208th General Assembly (1996) Presbyterian Church (U.S.A.), Louisville 1996; see pp. 78f, 110 ("moral and spiritual autonomy…social participation in defining and shaping the common good"); p. 104: "PRINCIPLE: Public participation that affects their lives [i.e of women, suffering from the additional "gender gap" in development) and well-being is a fundamental human right." So is participation in decision-making; pp. 120f: part of it is the recognition that the Spirit works in many cultures and religions. Not at least p. 123: "Christian expressions of people's suffering and struggles, articulated in 'people's theology' and so on, are appropriate, powerful forms of spirituality, which provide a foundation for the sustainability of their communities."

⁹ Kohler, note 3.7, pp. 135-140; G. Heitink, *Het diakenambt in de reformatorische kerken*, in: Praktische Theologie (NL), 1985/2, pp. 149-158; E.A. McKee, *Diakonia in the Classical Reformed Tradition and Today*, Grand Rapids 1989, p. 33, 45, 63; E.A. McKee, R.A. Ahonen, *Erneuerung des Diakonats als ökumenische Aufgabe*, Heidelberg 1996, notably pp. 128-140. In the Netherlands the deacon is still one of the three offices of the church: 'elder', 'deacon' and the professional 'minister of the Verbi Divini'. In other European countries, as far as I know, the formal office of deacon in a congregation does not exist. Elsewhere the situation varies widely. For the situation in the United States see the next note.

¹⁰ "The Diaconate is a spiritual office responsible for the ministry of mercy and stewardship of the congregation." So starts the passage on deacons in the Book of Order of the Presbyterian Church, U.S.A. (Ch. 3, III). Among the deacon's duties are "leading the congregation in discerning and ministering to needs such as… training the congregation in the use of the members' gifts in the ministry of mercy; offering family budget counseling; teaching principles

of giving." These very promising directives are overshadowed by another article: "A congregation by a majority vote may elect not to use the office of deacon. In such a case, or in the case where deacons cannot be secured, the function of the office shall always be preserved and shall devolve upon the elders
and the session" (G.6.0407). This is often the case in practice. It has to do with
the tradition and the difference between the two lay-offices. Elders are domi-
nant, for they govern the congregation, and consequently a board of deacons
often has conflicts with their 'governors' (J.S. Gray, J.C. Tucker, *Presbyterian
Polity for Church Officers*, Atlanta 1986, pp. 44-55). Along with Gray and
Tucker I prefer the ministry of service, grounded not only in compassion but
also in the concern for justice (ibid., 99ff). In *The Deacons Handbook. A man-
ual of Stewardship*, Grand Rapids 1980, the Reformed authors G. Berkhof and
L. de Koster give an overview of the office of the deacon in all churches, and
opt for a vision similar to mine – being Reformed too. In the Netherlands
elders and deacons together form the governing board, so there this problem
does not exist. Other problems, like how to realize effective social action, are
the same... See also note 3.9, McKee.

[11] See again the report on human development, *Hope for a Global Future*
(1996), note 3.10. In the twentieth century the ecumenical movement brought
a new, worldwide vision of diakonia, expressed recently in the document
Baptism, Eucharist and Ministry (1982). Another, even strong plea for diakonia
and indeed – as here – the primacy of diakonia in the church is made by
H. Haslinger, *Diakonie zwischen Mensch, Kirche und Gesellschaft. Eine praktisch-
theologische Untersuchung der diakonischen Praxis unter dem Kriterium des
Subjektseins des Menschen*, Würzburg 1996, pp. 749f. Haslinger made a diagram
consisting of three partly overlapping circles, which stand for leitourgia, marturia
and koinonia, surrounded by a much larger circle, overlapping the other ones:
diakonia. This, I would call "the diaconal congregation". However, I prefer the
notion of the congregation that is fundamentally involved in diakonia, but in
which not everyone is busy with this function of the church. The functions of
leitourgia and martyria should be related to diakonia, but each also has its own,
separate importance.

[12] H. Steinkamp, *Die sanfte Macht der Hirten. Die Bedeutung Michel Foucaults
für die Praktische Theologie*, Mainz 1999, esp. pp. 58ff. M. Foucault, *Histoire de la
sexualité*, tome 3, 'Le souci de soi', Paris 1984. Foucault uses classic philosophical
moral writings of the first centuries P.C., from Seneca (Stoa), Plutarchus and
Epictetus (pp. 60-85). *Aphrodisia*, the sexual love for women and boys, and other
pleasures of life must be fulfilled, but *mèden agan*, 'nothing too much'. Discussing
philosophy is, like Plato's meaning about this question, the highest aim of the love
for boys (224-261). Though everything is thought from a male perspective, mar-
riage is the only right place for heterosexual love (173-216). Moreover the

epimeleia seautou, the care for oneself, needs an ascetic way of living and is needed for good political and social conduct.

¹³ From our Handbook PT, pp. 593-602, and J.J. Ploeger-Grotegoed, *Diakonaat vanuit de ervaring,* in: Praktische Theologie (NL) 1991/4, pp. 441-460.

¹⁴ J.G. Kolk, Jaarverslagen (Annual reports) diakonaal consulent Hervormde Gemeente Arnhem, with telling titles like: *Looking with the eyes of the underdogs* (1985); *For lack of proof...guilty!* (1988); *Solidari-time* (1990); *Only because of your love the poor will forgive you that you give them bread* (1991) and the title, cited here, from 1989. Many of Kolk's insights have found their way implicitly into this chapter.

¹⁵ R. Houdijk, J. Pieper (eds.), *Dienst aan mensen.* Opstellen aangeboden aan Harry Spee ss.cc., Baarn 1995, pp. 14-28, here pp. 23ff.

¹⁶ G. Watson, "Resistance to Change", in: W.G. Bennis et al. (eds.), *The Planning of Change,* London, etc., 1970, pp. 488-498; J. Habermas, *Vorstudien und Ergänzungen zur Theorie des kommunikativen Handelns,* Frankfurt 1984, pp. 253ff; A.W. Gouldner, "Theoretical requirements of the applied social sciences", in: Bennis et al. 1970, pp. 85-98.

¹⁷ J.W. Skillen, *E Pluribus Unum and Faith-Based Welfare Reform: A Kuyperian Moment for the Church in God's World* (The Princeton Seminary Bulletin, 3/2001, pp. 285-305), makes a convincing argument for cooperation between State and Church in matters of social welfare in the United States, given that the state does not provide the level of facilities taken for granted in most Western European countries.

¹⁸ D.S. Browning, *A Fundamental Practical Theology. Descriptive and Strategic Proposals,* Minneapolis 1991, pp. 22-26.

¹⁹ K.A. Schippers, *De gemeente in de optiek van arbeid en geloof,* in: Praktische Theologie (NL) 1990/4, pp. 446-458.

²⁰ J. Moltmann, *Diakonie im Horizont des Reiches Gottes,* Neukirchen-Vluyn 1984, p. 14.

Chapter 4.

¹ Texts from the exhibition Diana Thater, *Knots + Surfaces* (2001/2002), Dia Center for the Arts, 548 West 22nd Street, New York.

² J. Burgers et al., "De verborgen stad. Een sociologische stadswandeling door Rotterdam", Amsterdam 2001. Part of the study by G. Engbersen, J. Burgers, *De verborgen stad. De zeven gezichten van Rotterdam,* Amsterdam 2001.
For an overview of multicultural problems see: J. Burgers, R. Kloosterman, "Dutch Comfort: Postindustrieller Uebergang und soziale Ausgrenzung in

Spangen, Rotterdam", in: W. Heitmeyer, R. Dollase, O. Backes (eds.), *Die Krise der Städte. Analysen zu den Folgen desintegrativer Stadtentwicklung für das ethnisch-kulturelle Zusammenleben*, Frankfurt 1998, pp. 211-232.

[3] N. Foner (ed.), *New Immigrants in New York* (rev. ed.), New York 2001, p. 16.

[4] R. Wright, M. Ellis, "Immigrants, the Native-Born, and the Changing Division of Labor in New York City", in: *New Immigrants*, note 4.3, pp. 81-110, here p. 106f.; P.R. Pessar, "Dominicans: Transnational Identities and Local Politics", in: *New Immigrants*, note 4.3, p. 254.

[5] J. Firet, J. Hendriks, *"I have nobody"*, s Gravenhage 1986.

[6] I owe these insights from Ina Nusselder in her master's thesis *Het zal ons een zorg zijn* (which has in Dutch the double meaning of "We will care" and "We should care"), Groningen, May 2002.

[7] U. Bach, *Boden unter den Füssen hat keiner. Plädoyer für eine solidarische Diakonie*, Göttingen 1986, p. 63.

[8] J.W. de Cruchy, *Christianity*, note 1.12, p. 1. See also A. Garcia-Rivera, *The Community of the Beautiful: A Theological Aesthetics*, Collegeville 1999, p. 182-186.

[9] Outsider Art Fair, January, 25-27, Sandford I. Smith, Soho, NYC; See the article by Ralph Blumenthal, "Success at 14, Despite Autism" (*New York Times*, January 16, 2002, E1,5) about a boy, Jonathan Lerman, with an IQ of 53 who from the age of 10, after the death of his grandfather, suddenly began to draw. Another example is the story of Hans Engelhart, a man with Down's Syndrome, the nephew of a Dutch performer, Herman Finkers, who makes wonderful paintings (Dutch Tv1, KRO-Kruispunt, December 2001).
I visited the Outsider Art Fair in New York. According to New York Times art critic Ken Johnson "dubious schlock is significantly reduced" and "more discriminating galleries mount the well-orchestrated displays". But now "there is a level of pictorial and technical ingenuity that is high by any standard", which raises the question: "Is it necessary to know if the artist is psychologically impaired? (…) It might be argued that outsider art should be defined not by the person who made it but by the nature of the work itself; call it extremely idiosyncratic art." "The outsider is a kind of Romantic hero, an escapee from the effects of social convention." Johnson concludes that the Outsider Art Fair "is also the celebration of a modern quasi-religious cult." Danto, "Outsider Art", in *The Madonna*, note 1.22, pp. 242ff, has about the same opinion. He quotes, assenting, Dubuffet: "There is no art of the insane any more than there is an art of dyspeptics or an art of people with knee complaints". I agree with them; the only difference I see is that there is not any postmodern artwork resting on sophisticated reasoning. I visited this fair to gather material about 'outsiders', the group my work focuses on, but ironically failed to find examples for the thesis of

my study, namely to show how important postmodern installations are for learning to understand the emotions of all kinds of outsiders.

[10] Tom Friedman tries to make his own observations and experiences into pictures and "anti-monumental" sculptures, by transforming the form and function of everyday materials like spaghetti, toothpaste, hair and pencil shavings. Exhibition 2001/2002 in the New Museum of Contemporary Art, New York.

[11] J. Beumer, *Reikhalzend*, Ten Have 1999, p. 15.

[12] S. Stoppels, *Gastvrijheid*, Kampen 1996, p. 283.

[13] H. Visser, *Op drift*, Amsterdam 1990, p. 116.

[14] H. Visser, *Creativiteit, wegwijzing en dienstverlening: de rol van de kerk in de postindustriële stad*, Zoetermeer 2000, p. 304.

[15] H. Visser, *Hopen tegen beter weten in. Verhalen en bezinning over de kerk in de stad*, Delft 1986, p. 38.

[16] G. van den Boomen, *De crypte is onze kerk. Tien jaar drugspastoraat*, Zoetermeer 2000; quotations from pp. 7, 33, 19 and 48.

[17] Dutch Tv1, KRO, Kruispunt, November 2001.

[18] A. Baart, "Verder dan het lege hart en de hoge borst", in: *Tijdschrift voor de sociale sector*, oktober 1999, p. 4-11. The following quotations are from the same article. In 2001 Baart presented the results of his research (see the next note).

[19] Baart, *Een theorie van de presentie*, Utrecht 2001, p. 273f.

[20] Baart, *Presentie*, note 19, p. 219. Actually, in principle – not in extension – exposure has much in common with the ways I try to teach church members to observe the need of people who are suffering.

[21] Each year about 40,000 foreigners – 0.25% of the total population of the Netherlands – request asylum. Twenty percent of these asylum-seekers will be expelled from the country within 48 hours; the remaining 80% are sent to a Refugee Center for at least six weeks, where they await the outcome of the preliminary investigation. In the case of a positive ruling, the asylum seeker goes to an official Asylum Center. The authorities have three years to make a final decision; most refugees are "urged to leave the Netherlands" (the majority of these will remain illegally in the EU) and only about 20% are given permission to stay in the country (Data from the Secretary of Aliens Policies; journal *Trouw*, 01-02-2002).

[22] Text at the video installation in the exhibition *Loop* in PS1.MoMA Contemporary Art Center, New York 2002.

[23] Lawrence Kohlberg is well known for his theory of the stages of moral development. He notes that modern Western governments think and act like a person at stage 4: mature but conventional ethical thinking. Statesmen may personally be at stage 5 (individual thinking, moderating one's own position) but in state affairs they act from the standpoint of stage 4. L. Kohlberg et al., *Lawrence Kohlberg's Approach to Moral Education*, New York 1989.

Chapter 5.

[1] Whitney Museum of American Art, New York, January, 2002, winter exhibition of work's from the museum's collection.

[2] Parts of this text are quotations from *World Views*, a hand-out by Moukhtar Kocache, for the exhibition at the New Museum of Contemporary Art in New York, winter 2001/2002.

[3] Quotations from Beuys, in: Joseph Beuys, *7000 Oaks*, Dia Center for the Arts, 548 West 22nd Street, New York.

[4] M. Rush, *New Media in Late 20th-Century Art*, London 1999.

[5] Whitney, 2002, winter exhibition on electronics and art. Part of the text from the guide.

[6] See note 4.22.

[7] Quotations from the curator of Dia Center for the Arts, Exhibition winter 2001/2002.

[8] C.S. Rabinowitz, "Displaced Delivery", in: M. ter Heijne, *Works*, Amsterdam 2000.

[9] Henk Boon, *De poeziezomer van Watou*, in HN, 25 August 2001, pp. 28f. To be clear, I did not attend the exhibition myself. I only give a comment on art critique.

[10] M. Seel, *Eine Aesthetik der Natur*, Frankfurt 1991, and the works mentioned in note 1.13.

Chapter 6.

[1] Paul Sztulman, *Short guide Documenta X*, Cantz Verlag, 1997, pp. 244f.

[2] Christel Vesters, Sam Taylor-Wood, in: Bulletin Stedelijk Museum Amsterdam, 1/2002.

[3] Sandra Spijkerman, Achter levenslust schuilt immense eenzaamheid, Trouw, 11-02-2002.

[4] P. Ricoeur, "On Interpretation", in: *From Text to Action. Essays in Hermeneutics*, II, Evanston 1991, pp. 1-20 (French: *Du texte à l'action*, Paris 1986); A.K. Ploeger, *Voortgaande transfiguratie* (Ongoing Transfiguration), inaugural lecture, Groningen, 13-09-1994.

[5] Janet Cardiff, *A Survey*, with walks in Louisiana, USA (1996), Münster, Germany (1997; figure 6.3), Villa Medici Walk in Rome (1998), Drogan's Nightmare for the XXIV Bienal de Sao Paulo (1998), The Missing Voice (1999); see pp. 63-69; 77-119. The one I walked was shown at the PS1.MoMA Contemporary Art Center, New York, winter 2001/2002.

LIST OF ARTISTS AND THEIR WORKS,

presented in this book

(between parentheses: the section)

Vito ACCONCI, *Other Voices for a Second Sight* (1974) (5.1)

Joseph BEUYS, *Strassenbahnhaltestelle (Tramstop Cleve, monument for the future)*, Kurhaus Kleve, 1947 (5.1)

Joseph BEUYS, *7000 Oaks*, Kassel 1982-1987; New York 2000 (Dia Center for the Arts) (5.1)

Mike BIDLO, *Not Andy Warhol*, 1991 (1.3)

Janet CARDIFF (Canada; collaboration with George Bures Miller), *The Dark Pool*, 1995 (2.4)

Janet CARDIFF, *To touch*, 1993 (1.4)

Janet CARDIFF, *Walk Münster*, 1997 (6.3)

Judy CHICAGO, *Dinner party*, 1974/1979 (2.5)

Carola DERTNIG, *Revolving Door*, World Views program Summer 2001 (5.1)

Jacqueline FRASER, *A Portrait of the Lost Boys, 'in five parts deftly and six details of straining'*, Courtesy of Roslyn Oxley Gallery, Sydney, 2001 (2.5)

Laurie HALSEY BROWN, *Between looking right (when remembering) and looking left (when creating)*, World Views program Summer 2001 (5.1)

Kara HAMMond, *Cenotaph*, World Views program Summer 2001 (5.1)

Ellen HARVEY, *Seeing Is Believing*, exposition *Surface*, 2002 (1.3)

Mathilde TER HEIJNE, *Life Inside Storage*, 2000 (5.2)

Michiel HUISMAN, *The Box*, 1998 (5.4)

Kiss and Tell, *Drawing the Line*, 1990 (2.5)

Job KOELEWIJN, *Het schoonmaken van het Rietveld Paviljoen* (Cleaning the Rietveld Pavilion), 1992 (2.2)

KOMAR & MELAMID, *Most Wanted Painting*, 1991 (1.3)

Geraldine LAU, *Information Retrieval*, World Views program Summer 2001 (5.1)

MASACCIO, *Holy Trinity*, Santa Maria Novella, Florence, 1427 (1.3)

Jorge PARDO & Gilberto ZORIO, *Reverb*, Dia Center for the Arts, 2001/2002 (5.1)

Walter PICHLER, *The Three Staffs*, Burgenland, Austia, 1997 (1.2; 1.5)

Michael RICHARDS, *Tuskeegee Airmen (destroyed)*, Twin Tower II, 11/09/2001 (5.1)

Fred SANDHURST, *Untitled*, 1987 (5.1)

Miriam SHARON, *The Desert People*, Ashoda Harbor, Tel Aviv, 1978 (3.1)

Santiago SIERRA, *Six People Who Cannot Be Paid for Sitting in the Interior of Cardboard Boxes*, Kunst-Werke Berlin, 2000 (4.5)

Regina SILVEIRA, *The Saint's Paradox*, Sao Paulo, about 1990 (5.4)

Nedko SOLAKOV, *A life (Black and White)*, PS1. Contemporary Art, 2002 (5.1)

Sam TAYLOR-WOOD, *Soliloqui III*, Stedelijk Museum Amsterdam, January 2002 (6.2)

Diana THATER, *Knots + Surfaces*, Dia Center for the Arts, 2001 (4.intro)

Andy WARHOL, *Brillo Box*, collection Jose Mugrabi, New York, 1964 (1.3)

Lois WEINBERGER (Austria), *Exotic Seeds Will Soon Overgrow the Indigenous Seeds*, Documenta X, Kassel 1997 (6.1)

David WOJNAROWICZ, *What's this Little Guy's Job in the World*, 1990 (5.1)

Lynne YAMAMOTO: *Untitled*, P.S.1 Contempory Art Center, New York 1998 (1.4)

Lynne YAMAMOTO, *Resplendent*, New York 2001 (1.4)

Ossip ZADKINE, De verwoeste stad (the Destruction of Rotterdam), 1952 (2.1)

LIST OF ILLUSTRATIONS

Cover

Figure 5.7. Mathilde Ter Heijne, *Life Inside Storage* (detail)

Chapter 1.

Figure 1.1a. Walter Pichler, *The Three Staffs and Floating Staff*
    1.1b. *House for the Three Staffs*, 3rd Project, 1997
    From: Walter Pichler, *Drawings: Sculptures: Buildings*,
    Stedelijk Museum Amsterdam 1998; ISBN 3851270193
Figure 1.2. Masaccio, *De trinità*, about 1425. Fresc, 667 x 317 cm.
    Florence, Santa Maria Novella.
Figure 1.3. Lynne Yamamoto, *Untitled*, P.S.1 Contempory Art Center, New York
    1998 (impression of the author; fragment)

Chapter 2.

Figure 2.1a, 2.1b, 2.1c. Ossip Zadkine, *De verwoeste stad* (The Destruction of
    Rotterdam)
Figure 2.2. Job Koelewijn, *Cleaning the Rietveld Pavilion*. Photo Koelewijn,
    from: *New Dutch Sculptors. Job Koelewijn*, published by New Sculpture
    Museum, Rijssen NL 1999, pp. 24f.
Figure 2.3. Job Koelewijn, Women in the traditional costume of Spakenburg.
    Photo Koelewijn, from: *New Dutch Sculptors. Job Koelewijn*, published by
    New Sculpture Museum, Rijssen NL 1999, p. 17
Figure 2.4. Janet Cardiff (collaboration with George Bures Miller), *The Dark
    Pool*, 1995, in: C. Christov-Bakargiev, *Janet Cardiff. A Survey of Works
    Including Collaborations with George Bures Miller*, PS1.MoMA, Long Island
    City 2001, p. 53
Figure 2.5. Kiss and Tell, Installation *Drawing the line*, 1990; Collective "Kiss
    and Tell", Vancouver; in: N. Stangos (ed.), *Concepts of Modern Art*, London
    1994, p. 138 (Photo Isabelle Massu 1990)

Chapter 3.

Figure 3.1. *Ground zero* (1991), photo by Nadine McGann from CNN's Operation Desert Storm, in: W.J.T. Mitchell, *Picture Theory*, Chicago & London 1994, p. 398

Figure 3.2. *Kaninchen und Ente*, from Fliegende Blätter (1892), in: Mitchell, p.55f.

Chapter 4.

Figure 4.1. Satellite TV dishes in a Rotterdam street aimed toward Morocco.

Figure 4.2. The Tovertunnel, a magic tunnel between two districts of Delfshaven.

Figure 4.3. The Tovertunnel, Delfshaven, with a view of the not yet renovated new town.

Figure 4.4. The Tovertunnel, Delfshaven, with a view of the renovated old town.

Figure 4.5a, 4.5b. Painting in the Trenton soupkitchen

Figure 4.6. "Thank you … for being there for me" (Trenton)

Figure 4.7. AZC Wolvega (NL), The First Exam

Chapter 5.

Figure 5.1 and 5.2. Joseph Beuys, *Strassenbahnhaltestelle* (*Tramstop*). Museum Kurhaus Kleve – Ewald Matare-Sammlung, Dauerleihgabe des Kroeller-Mueller-Museums, Otterlo (NL). Photoes: Annegret Gossens.

Figure 5.3. Joseph Beuys, *7000 Oaks* (here: the New York version)

Figure 5.4a, 5.4b. Solakov, *A life (Black and White)*

Figure 5.5. Mathilde ter Heijne, *Life inside storage*

Figure 5.6. Mathilde ter Heijne, *Life inside storage* (part of the installation)

Figure 5.7. Mathilde ter Heijne, *Life inside storage* (detail)

Figure 5.8. After Michiel Huisman, *The Box*

Chapter 6.

Figure 6.1. Sam Taylor-Wood, Soliloqui III, in: Bulletin Stedelijk Museum Amsterdam, 1/2002, p. 5

Figure 6.2. Wheelchair user at the post office

Figure 6.3. Collage of an open house

Figure 6.4a, 6.4b. Janet Cardiff's walk in Münster, in: C. Christov-Bakargiev, *Janet Cardiff. A Survey of Works Including Collaborations with George Bures Miller*, PS1.MoMA, Long Island City 2001, p. 86f